For Carolyn

Tiger Lily Publications Order of Battle Series

The Order of Battle Series is a distinct and authoritative series of studies of both historical and contemporary military history as viewed through the orders of battle, dispositions, and tables of equipment and organization of a particular force or country. We have taken advantage of recent advances in publishing technology to make available books that because of their narrow focus might in the past have been too costly to publish. All of our books are available in both print and e-book editions.

A list of published titles may be found on the back cover.

Please visit www.orbat.com or www.tigerlilybooks.com for more information.

Copyright © T. D. Shiflett
All illustrations are believed to be in the public domain.

All rights reserved. No part of this book may be copied, reproduced or transmitted in any form or by any means, electronic or mechanical, including photocopying, recording or by any information storage and retrieval system, without prior written permission of the publisher.

First published in 2006 by
Tiger Lily Publications
Takoma Park, MD
United States

Library of Congress Cataloging in Publication Data

ISBN 0-9776072-1-6

Table of Contents

America	*8*
Chippewa	*12*
Delaware	*14*
Franklin	*16*
Independence	*19*
New Hampshire	*27*
New Orleans	*32*
New York	*33*
North Carolina	*34*
Ohio	*37*
Pennsylvania	*42*
Vermont	*45*
Virginia	*50*
Washington	*51*
Tables	
Table 1 Summary of Service	*54*
Table 2 Comparison of the ships of the line	*55*
Table 3 Chronology of events	*56*
Glossary	*70*
Bibliography	*86*

Preface

Most published accounts of the United States of America's early sailing navy concentrate on either the construction of the ships or on their employment as instruments of sea power projection during the early years of the republic. Terry Shiflett has now produced a work which examines both of these approaches together and shows how the one influenced the other. Further enhancing our understanding of this era is an excellent glossary and a comprehensive chronology.

This work should be the definitive popular work on the early U.S. Navy for many years to come.

Lieutenant Commander Robert McArthur
United States Navy (retired)

Introduction

This book tells the story of the United States Navy's fifteen Ships-of-the-Line; ships which were the battleships of their day. These ships never gained glory fighting their equals in great fleet engagements such as Trafalgar or Copenhagen. Rather, they like the vast majority of warships ever built, performed their duties in a workmanlike manner by showing American naval might around the world, visiting foreign ports to facilitate American trade, and deterring aggression towards United States interests. It is perhaps understandable that they are now mostly forgotten. To understand the how and why as to the construction and operational history of these American ships, one must reach back to an even dimmer history and learn the roots from which all ships of the line sprang.

The classic definition of a ship-of-the-line is "a ship rigged warship with 64 or more guns on three or more decks which was large enough to take part in the main action of an engagement." The *Liner,* as these ships were colloquially referred to, evolved from the "Great Ships" such as the English *Henri-Grace-à-Dieu* of the early 1500's. From the standpoint of technology, these ships were a marked shift in English shipbuilding construction. They were carvel rather than clinker built and equipped with heavy guns mounted on a broadside near the waterline. They still had some of the awkward features of the old medieval round ship such as a high forecastle and poop, but these were less extreme than in the earlier ships.

Figure 1 - The Great Ship Henri-Grace-à-Dieu

The Great Ship *Henri-Grace-à-Dieu,* was laid down at Woolwich in October 1512 and launched in June 1514. She was approximately 165-feet long and displaced between 1000 and 1500 tons. The shipwrights had objected to cutting holes in the sides for the great guns, but the King was insistent. There was a risk in this; the other great gun ship built at this time, the *Mary Rose*, suddenly heeled over and sank when the water came through her lower gun ports on 19th of July 1545. *Henri-Grace-à-Dieu* mounted 80 guns, composed of almost every caliber in use. Of these 80 guns, 54 were pointed through broadside ports. The others were mounted, either as bow or stern chasers, or as "murdering pieces". The ship had four masts and was the first three-decked ship built in England.

The great ships evolved into galleons with smaller upper decks, increased speed and stability thus producing a type of ship useful for worldwide warfare. *Sovereign-of-the-Seas*, a classic ship of this type was built at Woolwich dockyard in 1637, by Mr. Phineas Pett. Subsequently renamed to *Royal Sovereign*, She was the most powerful ship of her time, and the first true three-decked ship built in England. Originally planned for 90 guns, she carried 102 when completed.

The decoration of the ship was designed by the playwright Thomas Heywood and made by John and Matthias Christmas at a total cost of £ 6691.

Figure 2 - Sovereign-of-the-Seas

Mr. Heywood recorded the appearance of *Sovereign-of-the-Seas*, "She has," says he, "three flush-deckes and a forecastle, an halfe-decke, a quarter-decke, and a round-house. Her lower tyre hath thirty ports, which are to be furnished with demi-cannon and whole cannon throughout, being able to beare them. Her middle tyre hath also thirty ports, for demi-culverin and whole culverin. Her third tyre bath twenty-size ports for other ordnance. Her forecastle hath twelve ports, and her halfe-decke hath fourteen ports. She hath thirteen or fourteen ports more within-board for murdering pieces, besides a great many loopholes out of the cabins for musket-shot. She carried, moreover, ten pieces of chase-ordnance in her right forward; and ten right aft, that is, according to land-service, in the front and the reare." Numbering the guns, we find 126 as the establishment of this first-rate of the seventeenth century.

It is probable that about the middle of the seventeenth century the practice of placing guns of a dissimilar caliber on the same deck was discontinued in the British Navy. This was a decided improvement since it brought an end to the delays and confusion caused by different size balls and powder charges on the same deck.

The division of the British navy into rates appears for the first time in 1626, was described as follows, "The new rates for seamen's monthly wages, confirmed by the commissioners of his majesty's navy, according to his majesty's several rates of ships, and degrees of officers." One fact is obvious, that the division into rates was adopted more to regulate the pay of the officers and seamen than it was to mark any distinction in the force or construction of the ships. The captain of every rate was paid differently. The same was also the case with many of the subordinate officers.

The first appearance of a classification by guns occurs in what purports to be "A list of all "shippes", "frigates", and other vessels belonging to the State's navy, on 1st March, 1651. The number of classes, or subdivisions by guns, comprised within the six rates, amounted to twenty-three.

The year1670 found the French navy to have consisted of five *rangs,* or rates, each composed of several *ordres,* or classes and that their first-class first-rates mounted 120 guns. The Dutch seem to have divided their navy into six rates. Their heaviest ships, of which there were but a few, are represented to have mounted 92 or 94 guns.

The characteristic of an English first-rate of 1677 seems to have been, "to mount her guns on three whole decks, a quarter-deck, forecastle, and poop; of a second-rate, to mount her guns on three whole decks and a quarterdeck; of a third-rate, to mount hers on two whole decks, a quarterdeck, forecastle, and poop ; of a fourth-rate, to mount hers on two whole decks and a quarterdeck."

The great naval wars of the 17th, 18th, and early 19th centuries, most notably the Anglo-Dutch Wars (1652-1654, 1665-1667, 1672-1674), accelerated the development of the most complex and deadly weapon of war invented up to that time - the ship-of-the-line. This type vessel was refined, as the early designs were tried in the crucible of battle, becoming larger, faster and less ornate as time and warfare continued.

Figure 3 - 64-gun ship London (1656)

London of 64 guns was a typical ship-of-the-line of the period; ornate and heavily gilded, she had a low forecastle, but retained a raised poop and quarterdecks.

In 1756, the British 50-gun ship, a 4th rate, being found too weak to stand in the line of battle, was reduced to an under-line class. The ship, however, although armed much in the same way as the two-decked 44, was not considered as a frigate, but continued to be called, as formerly, 50-gun ship. This left the 1st, 2nd, and 3rd rate ships to form the line of battle.

Thus, by the time the United States began designing ships-of-the-line in 1776 (*America*), and again in 1799, this class of ship had reached the pinnacle of development. It was not by a whim of a faceless bureaucrat that in 1813 directed that "ships to rate not less than 74 guns each" be constructed. The third rate ship of 74 guns had become the backbone of the European battle fleets, it had the near perfect combination of speed, maneuverability, and fighting power to dominate naval warfare. The American designs for the ships-of-the-line were at least partially influenced by the European model modified to meet the needs of a nation that had an extremely long coast line with a distinct lack of adequate deep water ports and facilities especially along the southern coasts. Whereas the ships-of-the-lines of England and France were to be used to project power world wide, the American ships role was that of a blockade breaker, with "cruizing" as a secondary role. These considerations, as well as limited experience in building such large ships and a wartime urgency to swiftly produce the vessels, resulted in an initial class of warships that were less then satisfactory when completed. Of these five wartime ships, two were never completed, one was cut down to a frigate, and the remaining two were swiftly laid up in ordinary as soon as the next class of ships became available.

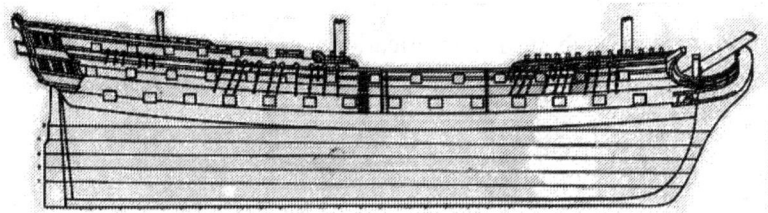

Figure 4 - Draught of the 74 gun ship Bellona

While Congress had authorized 74-gun ships in 1816 - 3rd rates in Europe, in practice American Captains were allowed to arm their ships as they pleased. The *Ohio* carried anywhere from 86 to 102 guns during her service, *North Carolina* also tended to be heavily over gunned for her rate, none the less, the ships were always carried on the Navy Roles as 74 gun ships. The *Chippewa, New Orleans* and *Pennsylvania,* each had their design changed during construction, producing ships capable of carrying upwards to 140 guns.

These ships proved to be a major improvement compared to their predecessors, to the point that *Ohio* could arguably be considered one of the best designed ships-of-the-line ever constructed. The expense of manning and maintaining such large ships in peace time forced these nine ships to remain on the stocks as a "fleet in being", as an economy effort, or if launched and commissioned, to spend a large amount of time in ordinary. When in active service they operated independent of each other, often as flagships on foreign stations, rather then as a battle fleet. Ultimately, the advent of shell firing guns, steam power and iron clad ships made the concept of sailing broadside-armed vessels obsolete.

The destruction of the three ships of the line at Norfolk Navy Yard in 1861 proved to be the death knell for them. The two remaining ships, still on the stocks in the north were launched to support the American Civil War, not as warships, but as floating auxiliary store and depot facilities.

Obsolete as warships, the three former line of battle ships remaining after the end of hostilities against the Confederate States in 1865, *Independence, New Hampshire,* and *Vermont,* continued to perform valuable service as receiving and training ships well in to the 20th century.

Note
___

Each entry is comprised of each ships specifications, as designed and as built, if different; a section on the vessels construction; a narrative history; and a source note.

The specifications section includes basic information about the vessel:

L/B/D:	Length, beam and draft or depth of the hold (dph.), the area of each measurement (i.e. waterline) will be noted, if known.
Tons:	Displacement (disp.)
Comp.:	Complement, broken down by Officers, crew, and marines, if known.
Arm.:	Armament, designed and actually carried, including the number of guns carried, the weight of shot, diameter of the projectile, or caliber of the bore. Long gun, carronade (carr.) or shell gun.
Des.:	The designer, builder, place and year laid down.
Launched:	The date the ship was launched.
Commissioned:	The Date the ship was formally commissioned.
Disposition:	The final fate of the ship.

America

The large landmass in the Western Hemisphere consisting of northern and southern continents.

L/B/D: 182'6" (upper gun deck); b. 50'6"; dph. 23'
Tons: 1,982
Comp.: 626 (total)
Arm.: 20 long 18-pdrs., 32 long 12-pdrs., 14 long 9-pdrs.
Des.: Designer: unknown, builder: John Langdon, Rising Castle (now Badger) Island in the Piscataqua River between
Portsmouth, N.H., and Kittery, Maine.
Laid down: May 1777
Launched: 5 Nov 1782
Commissioned: Never
Disposition: Transferred to France, June 1783. Broken up at Brest, France c.1786

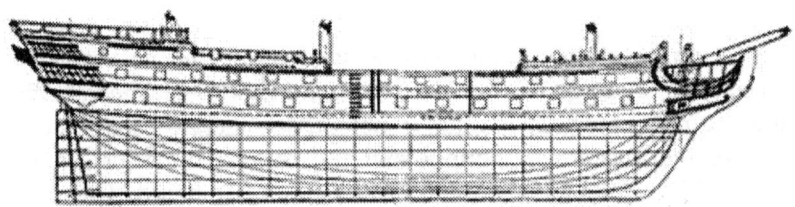

Figure 5 - Detail of the draught of the 74 gun ship, 1777 probably the official design for the American 74's projected by the Continental Congress..

On 9 November 1776, the Continental Congress authorized the construction of three 74-gun ships of the line. One of these men-of-war, *America*, was laid down in May 1777 in the shipyard of John Langdon on Rising Castle (now Badger) Island in the Piscataqua River between Portsmouth, N.H., and Kittery, Maine.

The *America* was, in her time, the heaviest ship that had ever been laid down on the continent for which she was named, and she was, also, the first ship of her class ever built by the Americans after their rebellion with England; and moreover, the only one of the three seventy-fours authorized that was built.

She had only single quarter galleries, and no stern gallery; and both stern and bows were made very strong, so that the men at quarters might be everywhere under good cover. The plan projected for the figurehead expressed dignity and simplicity. The head was a female figure, crowned with laurels. The right arm was raised, with forefinger pointing to heaven, as appealing to that high tribunal for the justice of the American cause. On the left arm was a buckler with a blue ground and thirteen silver stars. The legs and feet of the figure were covered here and there with wreaths of smoke to represent the dangers and difficulties of war. On the stern, under the windows of the great cabin, appeared two large figures in bas-relief, representing tyranny and oppression, bound and biting the ground, with the Cap of Liberty on a pole above their heads. On the back part of the starboard quarter gallery was a large figure of Neptune and on the starboard gallery was a large figure of Mars. Over the great cabin, on the highest part of the stern, was a large medallion, on which was a figure representing Wisdom surrounded by danger, with the bird of Athens over her head. Flashes of lightning probably emblematically expressed the danger surrounding Wisdom.

The *America* was fifty feet six inches in extreme breadth, and measured one hundred and eighty-two feet six inches on the upper gun deck. Yet this ship, though the largest of seventy-four guns in the world, had, *"when her lower battery was sunk, the air of a delicate frigate, and no person at the distance of a mile could have imagined that she had a second battery"*.

However, progress on her construction was delayed by a chronic scarcity of funds and a consequent shortage of skilled craftsmen and well-seasoned timber. The project dragged on for over two years under the immediate supervision of Col. James Hackett as master shipbuilder and the overall direction of John Langdon. Then, on 6 November 1779, the Marine Committee named Capt. John Barry as her prospective commanding officer and ordered him to *"hasten, as much as will be in your power, the completing of that ship."* Nevertheless, the difficulties, which previously had slowed the building of the warship, continued to prevail during the ensuing months, and little had been accomplished by mid-March 1780 when Barry applied for a leave of absence to begin on the 23d. However, he did perform one notable service for the ship.

A year and a half after she was authorized, on the 29th of May, 1778, the Marine Committee reported in favor of making her a razee two-decker, carrying twenty-eight twenty-four-pounders on the lower battery, and twenty-eight eighteen-pounders on the upper deck - in the whole fifty-six guns. This suggestion appears, however, not to have been adopted, after inspecting the unfinished vessel, which was slated to become his new command, Berry strongly recommended against the proposal, to reduce her to a 4th rate ship. His arguments carried the day, and the Marine Committee decided to continue the work of construction according to the ship's original plans.

All possibility of Barry's commanding *America* ended on 5 September 1780. He was ordered to Boston to take command of the finest ship ever to serve in the Continental Navy, the 36-gun frigate *Alliance*. She had recently arrived from Europe, her previous commander, Capt. Pierre Landais, a former officer of the French Navy, having being relieved for cause from that troubled ship.

Over nine months later, on 23 June 1781, Congress ordered the Continental Agent of Marine, Robert Morris, to get *America* ready for sea and, on the 26th, picked Capt. John Paul Jones as her commanding officer. Jones reached Portsmouth on 31 August and threw himself into the task of completing the man-of-war. Jones found the *America* - instead of being ready to be launched, as he had supposed - was not half built; and there was *"neither timber, iron nor any other material for finishing her."*. Money would not have procured the necessary articles of equipment and men before winter; but money was wanting; for the Navy Board at Boston had otherwise applied the funds which the Minister of Finance had destined for the *America*, and he found it impossible to make the necessary advances. The business of completing the ship began immediately, with some progress being made in construction before winter. It was a service not suited to his impatient temper, and Jones said that the task of inspecting her construction was *"the most lingering and disagreeable service he was charged with during the period of the Revolution"*.

As soon as the enemy had advice that there was a prospect of the *America* being finished, various schemes were suggested for her destruction, intelligence of which was sent in cipher to Portsmouth by the Minister of Marine. Jones applied to the government of New Hampshire for a guard to protect the vessel, and the Assembly voted to comply with his demand. None were however furnished, and on the second alarm sent by General Washington, the master builder, Mr. Hackett, and his associate were prevailed upon to mount guard with a party of carpenters by night. For some time Jones paid this guard himself, and took command of it in turn with the master builders. Large whale boats with muffled oars, full of men, came into the river, and passed and re-passed the America at night without daring to land.

When the birth of the Dauphin of France was officially communicated to Congress in the summer of 1782, several of the States celebrated the event with public rejoicing, and Jones seized the opportunity to *"testify the pleasure and gratitude"* - as he expressed it *"which he really felt"*. At his private expense, he had artillery mounted on board the *America*. She was decorated with the flags of different nations, displaying in front that of France; fired salutes as often as the forts, and thirteen royal salutes at a toast drunk at a public entertainment, and afterwards continued a 'feu de joie' until midnight. When it became dark, the vessel was brilliantly illuminated and displayed fireworks, which had a very fine effect, for it was a very dark night. The inhabitants of the town and its vicinity were assembled on the banks of the river, and testified their admiration by every possible show of applause. On the anniversary of our independence the same year, Jones, who was fond of show, made a similar rejoicing.

However, before the work was finished, Congress decided on 3 September 1782 to present the ship to King Louis XVI of France to replace the French ship of the line *Magnifique* which had run aground and been destroyed on 11 August 1782, while attempting to enter Boston harbor. The ship was also to symbolize the new nation's appreciation for France's service to and sacrifices in behalf of the cause of the American patriots.

This resolution was most disappointing to Jones, as this was the tenth command of which he had been deprived in the course of the Revolution. He continued, however, to urge forward the launch with the utmost energy. The difficulties were great. Langdon's Island was small, and between the stern and the opposite shore, Church hill, which was a continued rock, the distance did not exceed one hundred fathoms. From a few feet above the stern, a ledge of rocks projected far into the river, making an angle of twenty degrees with the keel; and from a small bay on the opposite shore, the flood tide continued to run with rapidity directly over this ledge, for more than an hour after it was high water by the shore. It was necessary to launch the ship exactly at high water, and to give her such a motion as would make her pass around the point of the ledges of rock without touching the opposite shore - then a difficult matter. When everything was prepared, Jones stood on the highest part of the prow. In this position, he could see her motion, and determine by a signal the instant when it was proper to let go one or both of the anchors that hung at the bows, and slip the end of the cable that depended on the anchor fixed in the ground on the island. The operation succeeded perfectly to his wish, and to the admiration of a large assembly of spectators.

After she had been rigged and fitted out, the ship-commanded by M. le Chevalier de Macarty Martinge, who had commanded *Magnifique* when she was wrecked-departed Portsmouth on 24 June 1783 and reached Brest, France, on 16 July. Little is known of her subsequent service under the French flag other than the fact it was brief. A bit over three years later, she was carefully examined by a survey committee which found her so damaged by dry rot as to beyond economical repair, probably caused by her wartime construction from green timber. She was accordingly scrapped and a new French warship bearing the same name was built.

Chippewa

Indian tribe of North America; Also, a battle won by the Americans on 5 July 1814 at Chippewa, Lake Ontario.

L/B/D: 204' (keel) ; b. 56'; dph. unknown
Tons: 2,805
Comp.: never manned
Arm.: 74-102 32pdr's
Des.: Designer: Henry Eckford , builder: Adam and Noah Brown, Sackett's Harbor, New York
Laid down: January 1815
Launched: Never
Commissioned: Never
Disposition: Uncompleted, sold 1 Nov 1833 and broken up.

Chippewa was the name assigned to one of two ships-of-the-line nearly completed in accordance with the act of 3 March 1813 which authorized the President *" . . . to have built, or procured, such a number of sloops of war, or other armed vessels, to be manned, equipped, and commissioned, as the public service may require, on the lakes . . .".*

She was laid down in January 1815 at Sackett's Harbor, Lake Ontario, N.Y., under terms of a contract let 15 December 1814 to Henry Eckford and Adam and Noah Brown. The contract provided that the *"master shipbuilders . . . will build or cause to be built as is hereafter set forth, two ships-of-the-line to carry from 74 to 100 guns each as Commodore Chauncey may direct, and one frigate of the largest class for use of the said United States, viz: Said vessels to be built at some proper place at Sackett's Harbor or its vicinity-and said Henry Eckford and Adam and Noah Brown do hereby promise to use every exertion in their power to have the said vessels ready to be launched in the spring or as early as the ice will permit and if possible by the 15th of May next . . .".*

By the spring of 1815 the Frantic naval arms race on which supremacy of Lake Ontario hinged had reached its peak, six hundred men were employed in her construction-the time between her keel being laid and preparation for launching was 42 days, an effort that typically took two or more years for comparable ships.

An active propaganda effort between Commodore Sir James Lucas Yeo of the Royal Navy's Lake Squadron and Commodore Chauncey resulted in the wide variance of reported size and number of guns to be carried by *Chippewa*. The

Office of the Board of Navy Commissioners noted: *Chippewa* was *"building at Sacketts Harbor when peace was concluded in consequence of which her further progress was arrested"*. *"...number of guns 87-to mount 63 long 32-pounders and twenty-four 32-pounder carronades...."*. The "Niles Weekly Register" of 18 March 1815 described *New Orleans* and *Chippewa* by reporting *...great progress in the building of a ship to carry 98 guns and another of 74 when the building was arrested by news of peace"*. A week later, the same publication described them as *"two lake monsters to carry 102 and 110 guns, now planked over"*. *Chippewa* remained on the stocks until sold for scrapping 1 November 1833.

Columbus

Christopher Columbus (Christobel Columbo), Adventurer from Genoa, in the service of Spain, was the first European to discover the West Indies.

L/B/D: 193' 3" ; b. 52'0"; dph. 21' 10"
Tons: 2,480
Comp.: 780
Arm.: 68 32pdr., 24 42pdr. Carr.
Des.: Designer: Doughty, builder: Doughty, Washington Navy Yard, Laid down: June 1816
Launched: 1 March 1819
Commissioned: 7 September 1819
Disposition: Sunk at Norfolk Navy Yard by withdrawing Union forces to prevent her falling into Confederate hands April 20 1861.

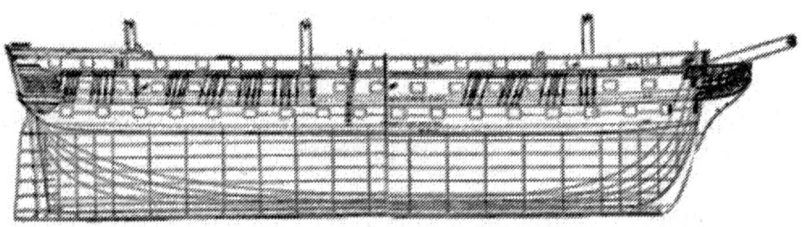

Figure 6 - Draught of the 74-gun ship Columbus 1815.

The *Columbus*, the second ship so named, rated as a 74 gun ship of the line, was launched 1 March 1819 by Washington Navy Yard and commissioned 7 September 1819. Her design was considered the most successful of her type constructed during the war of 1812. However, as with the other wartime "liners", she was unable to carry her lower gun deck high enough above the water when in a service condition. To prevent the ship from swamping in rough weather, the lower gun ports had to be closed, reducing her weight of shot thrown by nearly a third. That the ship could not comfortably carry her designed armament on her displacement tonnage was a direct design policy that all ships should have the heaviest armament possible in a given rate.

As Doughty pointed out, the unusually heavy armament of the American ships of the line made comparisons to foreign ships of the same nominal rating highly misleading. It was accepted that the American ships could either show less freeboard then foreign liners, with the official complement of guns aboard, or could show more by reducing their armaments - which even then would leave the American ships superior in force to European ships. The full compliant of guns were retained onboard *Columbus* as her dimensions were so much larger compared to the European ships.

Responding to the excitement generated by the pending launch of Columbus, the Commandant of Washington Navy Yard distributed the following flyer: "Navy yard, Washington, February 26, 1819. The opinion which had been entertained, that such of the inhabitants of the District and its vicinity, as also such strangers who are now sojourning with us, as may be desirous of seeing the Launch of the Ship of the Line, would have been furnished, in due time, with tickets of admission, has been found to be impracticable. As it is intended only to exclude disorderly persons, notice is hereby given, that all others, inhabitants and strangers, will be admitted on presenting themselves at the gate. The weather and tide admitting, it is expected the launch will take place about 10 o'clock on Monday morning, the 1st of March Thomas Tingey, Commandant."

Master Commandant J. H. Elton in command, she departed Norfolk, Va., 28 April 1820. *Columbus* served as flagship for Commodore W. Bainbridge in the Mediterranean until returning to Boston 23 July 1821. Serving as a receiving ship after 1833, she remained at Boston in ordinary until sailing to the Mediterranean, 29 August 1842, as flagship for Commodore C. W. Morgan. On 24 February 1843, she sailed from Genoa, Italy, and reached Rio de Janeiro, Brazil, 29 July to become flagship of the Brazil Squadron, Commodore D. Turner. She returned to New York 27 May 1844 for repairs.

After embarking Commodore J. Biddle, Commander East Indies Squadron, she sailed 4 June 1845, for Canton, China, where on 31 December, Commodore Biddle exchanged ratified copies of the first American commercial treaty with China. *Columbus* remained there until April 1846 when she sailed for Japan to attempt opening Japan to American commerce. She raised Tokyo Bay 19 July in company with USS *Vincennes*, an eighteen-gun sloop of war, but achieved no success. Recalled at the outbreak of the Mexican War *Columbus* reached Valparaiso, Chile, in December and arrived off Monterey, Calif., 2 March 1847. Too large to be useful in the California operations do to a lack of deep water ports, the ship sailed from San Francisco 25 July for Norfolk, arriving 3 March 1848. At Norfolk Navy Yard, *Columbus* lay in ordinary until 20 April 1861 when she was sunk by withdrawing Union forces to prevent her falling into Confederate hands.

Delaware

An Indian tribe, a state of the United States, a bay, and a river.

L/B/D: 196'3"; b. 54'4"; d. 26'2"
Tons: 2,633
Comp.: 820
Arm.: 74 32pdr
Des.: Designer: Doughty, builder: Norfolk Navy Yard
Laid down: August 1817
Launched: 21 October 1820
Commissioned: 27 March 1827
Disposition: Burned 20 April 1861 at Norfolk Navy Yard, along with other ships and the yard facilities to prevent their falling into Confederate hands.

Figure 7 - USS Delaware Detail of oil by Rear Admiral J. W. Schmidt

Delaware, a ship-of-the-line, was laid down at Norfolk Navy Yard in August of 1817 and launched 21 October 1820. Her design was a slight improvement of the wartime 74's, she and *North Carolina*, her sister were in fact in weight of shot thrown as powerful as many British liners of 120 guns. She was considered a fast sailer, making 12 knots in strong winds.

Figure 8 - The Launching of USS Delaware 21 October 1820

Roofed over, she was kept at the yard in ordinary until ordered repaired and fitted for sea in March 1827. *Delaware* put to sea 10 February 1828 under the command of Captain J. Downs to become the flagship of Commodore W. I. M. Crane in the Mediterranean. Arriving at Algeciras Bay, Spain, 23 March, she served in the interests of American commerce and diplomacy in that area until returning to Norfolk 2 January 1830

Decommissioned 10 February 1830, she lay in ordinary at Norfolk until 1833. On 17 June 1833, she became the first ship in North America to be dry-docked. Recommissioned 15 July, she received President Jackson on board 29 July, firing a 24-gun salute at both his arrival and departure. The following day she set sail for the Mediterranean where she served as flagship for Commodore D. T. Patterson, cruising on goodwill visits including stops in the Holy Land for the protection of the rights and property of American citizens until her return to

Hampton Roads, 16 February 1836. She was placed in ordinary from 10 March 1836 until recommissioned 7 May 1841 for local operations from Norfolk.

Delaware sailed 1 November 1841 for a tour of duty on the Brazil Station as flagship for Commodore C. Morris. She patrolled the coasts of Brazil, Uruguay, and Argentina to represent American interests during political unrest in those countries. On 19 February 1843, she sailed from Rio de Janeiro for another cruise in the Mediterranean. Returning to Hampton Roads 4 March 1844 she was decommissioned at Norfolk Navy Yard on the 22nd.

Still in ordinary there in 1861, she was burned 20 April along with other ships and the yard facilities to prevent their falling into Confederate hands.

Figure 9 - Bronze Replica of USS Delaware's Figurehead, USNA

In June 1930, the Class of 1891 presented a bronze replica of *Delaware's* figurehead to the United States Naval Academy. This bust, one of the most famous relics on the campus, has been widely identified as that of Native American leader of the Shawnee people, Tecumseh. However, when it adorned the man-of-war, it commemorated not Tecumseh but Tamanend, the revered Delaware chief who welcomed William Penn to America when he arrived in Delaware country on 2 October 1682.

The original figurehead was an elaboration of traditional figurehead style combined with 19th century realism; it was carved in 1820 by William Luke of Portsmouth, Virginia. The Bust was technically accomplished and academic rather then a folk art manner.

Franklin

Benjamin Franklin (1706-90). During the Revolution he was appointed American Minister Plenipotentiary to the French Court enabling him to function also as the Navy's representative in Europe.

Figure 10 - Period etching of USS Franklin

L/B/D: 187' 10 ¾"; b 50'0"; dph. 19'9"
Tons: 2,257
Comp.: 820
Arm.: 63 long 32-pdrs, 24 32-pdr carronades
Des.: Designer: Samuel Humpherys , builder: Humpherys and Penrose,. Philadelphia Navy Yard
Laid down: May 1813
Launched: August 1815
Commissioned: October 1815
Disposition: Broken up at Portsmouth, NH 1852

The third *Franklin*, a ship-of-the-line, built in 1815 under the supervision of Samuel Humphreys, was the first vessel to be laid down at the Philadelphia Navy Yard.

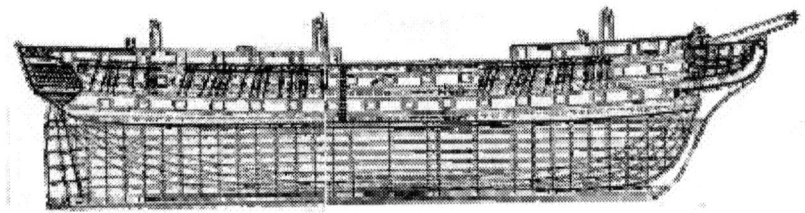

Figure 11
Draught of the 74-gun ship Franklin, showing alterations made in the original design.

As designed, her appearance was similar to the 1799 74-gun ship design of Joshua Humphreys, however she was 4 feet longer and no longer sported the rounded bow of those proposed ships. She, like *Columbus*, *Washington* and *Independence* suffered from the inability to carry her designed armament high enough above water when carrying her service complement and stores. This may have been alleviated had the ships carried progressively lighter guns on the higher tiered gun decks as was the norm in European ships of the line, however the prevailing philosophy in the American naval community, based on war time experience was that ships should carry the maximum number of guns for their rate, and of a uniform caliber.

Franklin sailed on her first cruise on 14 October 1817. Under the command of Master Commandant H.E. Ballard she proceeded from Philadelphia to the Mediterranean. She carried the Hon. Richard Rush, U.S. Minister to England, to his post. Subsequently she was designated flagship of the Mediterranean Squadron, cruising on that station until March 1820. She returned to New York on 24 April 1820.

From 11 October 1821 until 29 August 1824 she served as flagship on the Pacific Station. *Franklin* was laid up in ordinary until the summer of 1843 when she was ordered to Boston as a receiving ship. She continued in this capacity until 1852 at which time she was taken to Portsmouth, N.H. and broken up.

Independence

Freedom of control by others; self-government.

Figure 12 - Detail of painting of USS Independence, starboard side, 1815, NARA

L/B/D: 190'10"; 54' 7"; 21'4 (Ship of the Line)
188'0"; 51'6", 14' 10" dph (1836 Razee)
Tons: 2,243 (Ship of the line)
     1,891 (1836 Razee)
Comp.: 790 (Ship of the Line)
     750 +/- (1836 Razee)
Arm.: 30 long 32pdrs 33 medium 32pdrs 24 32pdr carr. (Designed)
     8 8" shell guns 48 32pdrs. (1848)
Des.: Designer: William Doughty builder: Hartt & Barker, Charlestown
Laid down: May 1813
Launched: 22 June 1814
Commissioned: July 1814
Disposition: 20 September 1919, burned on the Hunter's Point (San Francisco, CA) mud flats to recover her metal fittings.

Independence, first ship-of-the-line commissioned in the U.S. Navy, launched 22 June 1814 in the Boston Navy Yard. Taking on guns & stores and she was stationed with frigate *Constitution* to protect the approaches to Boston Harbor.

Considered to be the worst design of the war ship's of the line, *Independence* showed only 3' 10" between her water line and the sill of her gun ports amidships. This largely do to the ill-advised modifications made by Commodore William Bainbridge during her construction, coupled with the prevailing mania of the senior naval officers to heavily over gun ships of all types then prevalent in the US Navy. This severely degraded her usefulness as a ship of the line, as her lower battery could not be used in any but the calmest seas.

Wearing the broad pennant of Commodore William Bainbridge, and under command of Captain William Crane, she led her squadron from Boston 3 July 1815 to deal with piratical acts of the Barbary Powers against American merchant commerce.

A squadron under Decatur had enforced peace by the time *Independence* arrived in the Mediterranean were she led an impressive show of American naval might before Barbary ports that encouraged them to keep the peace treaties concluded. Having served adequate notice of rising U.S. sea power and added to the prestige of the Navy and the Nation, *Independence* returned to Boston 15 November 1815.

Figure 13 - Sail plan of Ship of the Line USS Independence 1815, NARA

In April 1817, Doughty recommended do to her obvious faults, she be razeed to a two-deck frigate or a 60 gun ship, removing her spar deck entirely, however nothing was done with this proposal for another 18 years.

She continued to wear the broad pennant of Commodore Bainbridge at Boston until 29 November 1819, and then, still in Boston, flagship of Commodore John Shaw until placed in ordinary in 1822.

Independence remained in ordinary at Boston until 1836 when she was placed in dry dock #1 and razeed or cut down to one covered fighting deck with poop and forecastle. She was rated down to 54 guns as her configuration gave way to that of a very large frigate. She proved to be one of the fastest and most powerful "frigates" of the US Navy, retaining the scantlings and heavy masts of a ship of the line on far less tonnage, while carrying one of the heaviest broadsides of a 5th rate ship in the world. It was felt she could defeat any frigate or lesser ship she might meet, while being able to out run any vessel capable of defeating her. This theory was however never put to test during her remaining sixty-six years in commission.

Recommissioned 26 March 1837 she sailed from Boston 20 May 1837 as flagship of Commodore John B. Nicholson. On board for her record passage across the Atlantic to England was the Honorable George Dallas, Minister to Russia. She arrived at Portsmouth, England, 13 June, called at Copenhagen; and then proceeded into Kronstadt 29 July 1937 to receive a visit from the Emperor of Russia. Two days later, a steamboat arrived to transport Mr. Dallas and his family to St. Petersburg.

Figure 14 - A Period painting of Independence as a razee. NARA

Having received marked social courtesies from the Russian government, *Independence* departed Kronstadt 13 August 1837 for Rio de Janeiro, where she became flagship of the Brazil Squadron to guard American commerce along the eastern seaboard of South America. This duty continued into the spring of 1839 when Commodore Nicholson attempted mediation to end the war between France and Argentina. He reported 22 April 1839 that: *"I volunteered, as I conceived it a duty I owed to my Country, as well as to all Neutrals, to endeavor to get peace restored that commerce should be allowed to take its usual course. In accordance of the feelings of humanity at least, I hope my endeavors will be approved by the Department . . . I see no probable termination of this War and Blockade which is so injurious to the Commerce of all Neutrals ...
"*

Independence returned north to New York 30 March 1840. She was laid up in ordinary until 14 May 1842 when she became flagship of Commodore Charles Stewart in the Home Squadron. Basing at Boston and New York, she continued as his flagship until laid up in ordinary 3 December 1845. She recommissioned 4 August 1846 and the Nation was at war with Mexico as she departed Boston 29 August 1846 for the coast of California. She entered Monterey Bay 22 January 1847 and became the flagship of Commodore William B. Shubrick, commanding the Pacific Squadron.

Independence assisted in the blockade of the Mexican coast, capturing Mexican ship *Correo* and a launch 16 May 1847. She was present to support the capture of Guaymas 19 October and landed blue jackets and Marines to occupy Mazatlan 11 November 1847, suffering the following casualties:
> Killed:
> Seaman Peter Johnson
> Wounded:
> Lt. H. A. Wise; slightly, edge of left scapula.
> Passed Midshipman W. D. Austin; slightly, ball grazing left hand.

She later cruised as far as Hawaii, arriving Honolulu 12 August 1848. *Independence* returned to the East Coast at Norfolk 23 May 1849 and decommissioned there 30 May.

Recommissioned 7 July 1849, *Independence* departed Norfolk 26 July under Captain Thomas A. Conover to serve as flagship of the Mediterranean Squadron under Commodore Charles W. Morgan. She was the first U.S. man-of-war to show the flag at Spezia, Italy, arriving 23 May 1850 for an enthusiastic welcome. Returning to Norfolk 25 June 1852 she was placed in ordinary at New York 3 July 1852.

Independence recommissioned September 1854 and departed New York 10 October to serve as flagship of the Pacific Squadron under Commodore William

Mervine. She arrived Valparaiso, Chile, 2 February. Her cruising grounds ranged northward to San Francisco and west to Hawaii. Proceeding from Panama Bay, she entered the Mare Island Navy Yard 2 October 1857, where she served as receiving ship there until decommissioned 3 November 1912. Her name was struck from the Navy List 3 September 1913.

Independence did not leave the Mare Island Navy Yard until 28 November 1914. Sold to John H. Rinder, she was towed to the Union Iron Works, San Francisco. On 5 March 1915 she shifted to Hunter's Point, and remained for a week. Some repairs were made and a plan formulated to use her as a restaurant for the Panama-Pacific Exposition. However, this plan was not executed though a permit was granted by Exposition authorities. Pig iron and ballast were removed from her hold and valuable hard wood salvaged from her orlop deck knees. The night of 20 September 1919, *Independence* was burned on the Hunter's Point mud flats to recover her metal fittings. The veteran of the days of wooden ships and iron men had survived more than a century, 98 years of which were spent serving the U.S. Navy.

The "San Francisco Chronicle, of November 20, 1912" printed the following article about the Independence's decommissioning and possible fate.
<u>FLAG LOWERED ON OLDEST FRIGATE?</u>
Historic Ship Independence is Placed out of Commission at Mare Island.
CALLED "NAVAL ARGONAUT."

Figure 15 - USS Independence as a receiving ship, Mare Island

Movement on Foot to Preserve Relic as an Exhibit for 1915 Exposition. Special Dispatch to the "Chronicle." Vallejo, November 19. —The historic old frigate *Independence*, for the past fifty-four years receiving ship at Mare Island and the oldest ship in the United States Navy, was placed out of commission at Mare Island this morning. The ceremony of hauling down the flag was a simple one, and the men and property were formally transferred to the more modern cruiser *Cleveland*, lately returned from Nicaragua.

Just what will be done with the *Independence* has not as yet been officially announced. It has been frequently reported that the directors of the Panama-Pacific Exposition would make some arrangements with the Government whereby the relic of another century would become one of the exhibits in 1915. As yet official word to this effect has never been received here.

Prominent Native Sons and Daughters of the Golden West have petitioned the Government to retain the *Independence* because of its association with the early history of California. For that reason it has often been referred to as "the naval Argonaut," it having first sailed up the coast in 1846, before the days of gold.

The keel of the *Independence* was laid down at Boston in 1812, it having been the intention of the Navy Department to have the ship ready for the war with England in that year. However, unfortunate delays occurred and the *Independence* was not launched until 1814, when as the flagship of Commodore Bainbridge it took a prominent part in the war against Algiers.

In 1836, the frigate was still the pride of the old white navy, and to keep it up-to-date it was cut down to three stacks [from 3 to 2 decks], and the guns reduced from seventy-four to fifty-four. At this time, the *Independence* was good for ten knots an hour in the wind, which was considered very fast time.

In 1846, commanded by Commodore Shubrick, the Independence paid its first visit to California, having come around the horn to harass the Mexican coast, at the time of the war with that country. Returning to the east coast, the frigate became the flagship of the European squadron. It returned to this coast eight years later and has been at Mare island ever since.

The old frigate displaces 3700 tons [note incorrect tonnage], which is one-tenth of the displacement of the new *Pennsylvania [(BB-38)]*. Its value at this time is in the [sic] brass used in its make up. At that time, copper was a cheap metal, and every bolt, rivet and rod on the *Independence* is of that mineral.

New Hampshire

New Hampshire, 9th of the original colonies to enter the Union, ratified the Constitution 21 June 1788.

Figure 16 - USS New Hampshire, receiving ship Newport RI. NARA

Other names Used: Alabama (original name), Granite State (renamed 30 November 1904)
L/B/D: 196' 3"; 53' 6"; 21' 6" dph
Tons: 2,633
Comp.: 820 (as a ship of the Line)
Arm.: 74 32pdr (designed) 4 100pdr, 6 9" shell guns (stores ship)
Des.: Designer: builder: Portsmouth Navy Yard, N. H.
Laid down: June 1819
Launched: 23 April 1864
Commissioned: 13 May 1864
Disposition: Sold for scrap, while under tow to the Bay of Fundy, the towline parted during a storm, she caught fire and sank off Half Way Rock in Massachusetts Bay on July 26 1922.

New Hampshire was originally to be the 74-gun ship of the line *Alabama* but remained on the stocks for nearly 40 years, well into the age of steam, before being renamed *New Hampshire* (The State of Alabama having seceded from the Union) and launched as a stores and depot ship during the American Civil War.

As *Alabama*, she was one of *"nine ships to rate not less than 74 guns each"* authorized by Congress 29 April 1816, and was laid down by the Portsmouth Navy Yard, New Hampshire, in June 1819, the year the State of Alabama was admitted to the Union. Though ready for launch by 1825, she remained on the stocks for preservation; an economical measure that avoided the expense of manning and maintaining a ship of the line.

Like her near sisters, Delaware and North Carolina, she originally was to have curved upper head rails popular at the start of the War of 1812, but the straight rails introduced into the Royal Navy much earlier as a matter of wartime economy, were installed on all of these ships after 1820. Smaller and having a lesser depth then *Ohio* (designed by Eckford), she would have carried her designed complement of guns a good deal lower. Designed to be an improvement on the wartime liners, these ships were in fact only slightly improved over *Columbus*, the best of the previous class, being fast sailors and of stronger construction, they were deemed acceptable and the design not altered.

Renamed *New Hampshire* 28 October 1863, she was launched 23 April 1864, fitted out as a stores and depot ship of the South Atlantic Blockading Squadron, and commissioned 13 May 1864, Commodore Henry K. Thatcher in command. *New Hampshire* sailed from Portsmouth 15 June and relieved sister ship *Vermont* 29 July 1864 as store and depot ship at Port Royal, South Carolina, and served there through the end of the Civil War. Her cavernous holds and gun decks, bereft of most of her armament were ideal for her new role. Care had to be taken in her handling when in a light condition as she road well above her designed draft, making her very unweatherly.

She returned to Norfolk on 8 June 1866, serving as a receiving ship there until 10 May 1876 when she sailed back to Port Royal. She resumed duty at Norfolk in 1881 but soon shifted to Newport, Rhode Island. She became flagship of Commodore Stephen B. Luce's newly formed Apprentice Training Squadron, marking the commencement of an effective apprentice-training program for the Navy. As a receiving ship, she was fitted with a deckhouse aft of the foremast to just forward of the mizzen. Her running rigging and sails were removed, leaving only standing rigging to support her masts.

New Hampshire was towed from Newport to New London, Connecticut, in 1891 and was receiving ship there until decommissioned 5 June 1892. The following year she was loaned as training ship for the New York State Naval Militia, which was to furnish nearly a thousand officers and men to the Navy during the Spanish-American War.

Figure 17 - Group of New York Naval Reserves on USS New Hampshire 1901
Detroit Publishing Co. no. 021426

New Hampshire was renamed *Granite State* 30 November 1904 to free the name "New Hampshire" for a newly authorized battleship (BB-25). Stationed in the Hudson River, *Granite State* continued training service throughout the years leading to World War I when state naval militia were practically the only trained and equipped men available to the Navy for immediate service. They were mustered into the Navy as National Naval Volunteers. Secretary of the Navy Josephus Daniels wrote in his Our Navy at War: *"Never again will men dare ridicule the Volunteer, the Reservist, the man who in a national crisis lays aside civilian duty to become a soldier or sailor - they fought well. They died well. They have left in deeds and words a record that will be an inspiration to unborn generations."*

On 23 May 1921, the *Granite State* was severely damaged by fire, while tied to the 96th Street Pier in New York City. Oil, pooling around the ship from a leaking six-inch Standard Oil Company pipe, was ignited from the backfire of a passing captain's gig. The resulting fire, aggravated by low water pressure on shore, destroyed the gig, a three-story naval office, storehouse and the *Granite State*. Before the crew abandoned ship, they flooded the vessel's powder magazine, preventing an explosion that would have devastated the surrounding area. Fireboats pumped tons of water into the flaming hulk until it settled into the mud. Listing sharply to port, the vessel was kept from capsizing only by its mooring chains.

Figure 18 - Burned out hulk of Granite State, New York Harbor, 23 May 1921
Massachusetts Board of Underwater Archaeological Resources

On 19 August 1921, the burned out hulk of the *Granite State* was sold at auction for $5000 the Mulholland Machinery Corporation. It was estimated that $70,000 of salvageable material could be removed from the wreckage, which was fastened and sheathed with over 100 tons of copper. Two five-ton anchors, along with 100 tons of chain, were still aboard the vessel. In addition, it was rumored that the ship's keel contained three gold spikes. Thus, a five month salvage operation was undertaken after which the lower gun ports were sealed with canvas patches, the water pumped out and the hulk was taken in tow for Eastport, Maine, where it was to be broken up.

While under tow by the tug *Perth Amboy*, five days out of New York City, a fire of undetermined origin broke out on board the hulk. Starting around 10AM and spreading quickly, the small salvage crew was forced to abandon ship, just as the towline parted from the flaming bow and the hulk was adrift. The intense fire forced the *Perth Amboy* to stand off helplessly, unable to secure a new tow or even fight the fire. At midnight, observers on shore saw the flames suddenly go out. The former warship had fetched atop the granite shoals on the southwest corner of Graves Island where beyond recovery, the vessel was slowly battered to pieces by wind and sea.

Figure 19 - Wreck of Granite State, Graves Island, Mass. 19 August 1921
Massachusetts Board of Underwater Archaeological Resources

Three salvage operations recovered huge oak timbers from the wreck for the copper with which they were fastened. Over the years, one of *New Hampshire's* anchors and numerous cannon balls have reportedly been recovered. The November 2, 1965 edition of the "Boston Globe" reported that Norwood resident William Kolb planned on recovering artifacts from the vessel while he was manning the "Aqua Cabin" underwater habitat, which was placed in 80 feet of water a short distance form the wreck site by the Hektor Scientific Company of Foxboro, Massachusetts. The shipwreck is in 30 ft (9 m) of water, and is an easy scuba dive. Although the hull is mostly buried in the sand, small artifacts and copper spikes may still be found. Location: Graves Island, Manchester Coordinates: Latitude - 42°-34'-16" N Longitude - 70°-44'-45" W

New Orleans

A city in the state of Louisiana. New Orleans was founded in 1718 by Jean Baptiste Le Moyne, sieur de Bienville, and named for the regent of France, Philipp II, duc d'Orleans

L/B/D: 204' (keel), 56', 26'
Tons: 2,805
Comp.: never manned
Arm.: 63 long 32pdrs., 24 32pdrs carr. (Initially) up to 130 (proposed)
Des.: Designer: Eckford, builder: Adam and Noah Brown, Sacketts Harbor, N.Y.
Laid down: January 1815
Launched: never
Commissioned: never
Disposition: sold 24 September 1883 to H. Wilkinson, Jr., of Syracuse, N.Y., broken up on the stocks

Figure 20 - USS New Orleans on the stocks, Sacketts Harbor NY

It is possible that the first *New Orleans* was never launched. During the War of 1812, there was a shipbuilding race on Lake Ontario, She was laid down in January 1815 by Henry Eckford and Adam and Noah Brown at Sacketts Harbor, N.Y. She was run-up and ready for launch in less then three months, an effort that typically took well over a year in ordinary times. Do to the ongoing propaganda campaign surrounding her construction, she was reputed to have been designed to carry anywhere from 90 to 130 guns. Her building was halted upon conclusion of peace with Great Britain, and she remained on the stocks, housed over, until sold 24 September 1883 to H. Wilkinson, Jr., of Syracuse, N.Y.

New York

A State in New England, one of the original 13 colonies.

L/B/D: 196'3"; b. 54'4"; d. 26'2"
Tons: 2,633
Comp.: 820
Arm.: 74 32pdr
Des.: Designer: Doughty, builder: Norfolk Navy Yard
Laid down: 1820
Launched: Never
Commissioned: Never
Disposition: Burned 20 April 1861 at Norfolk Navy Yard, along with other ships and the yard facilities to prevent their falling into Confederate hands.

The third *New York*, laid down in 1820 and was of the same class as *Delaware* and *North Carolina*, but never left the stocks. She was burned in April 1861 at Norfolk Navy Yard in Portsmouth, Virginia to keep her from falling into Confederate hands as the Federal forces abandoned the State of Virginia.

North Carolina

One of the thirteen original states.

Figure 21 - USS North Carolina-Detail of oil by Rear Admiral J. W. Schmidt

L/B/D: 196'3"; b. 53'6"; d. 26'2"
Tons: 2,633
Comp.: 820
Arm.: 74 32pdr (as authorized)
Pierced for 102 (as built)
82 42pdrs long guns, 12 32pdr carronades (as Commissioned)
56 42pdrs, 26 32pdr carr, and 8 8" shell guns (1856)
Des.: Designer: Doughty, builder: Philadelphia Navy Yard
Laid down: 1818
Launched: 7 September 1820
Commissioned: 24 June 1824
Disposition: Sold at New York 1 October 1867 for $30,000 and broken up

The first *North Carolina* was laid down in 1818 by the Philadelphia Navy Yard; launched 7 September 1820; and fitted out in the Norfolk Navy Yard. Master Commandant Charles W. Morgan was assigned to *North Carolina* as her first commanding officer 24 June 1824.

Her design was a slight improvement of the wartime 74's, as she carried her lower guns high enough above the water line to be useful in heavy seas, she and *Delaware*, her sister were in fact in weight of shot thrown as powerful as many British liners of 120 guns.

Considered by many the most powerful naval vessel then afloat, *North Carolina* served in the Mediterranean as flagship for Commodore John Rodgers from 29 April 1825 until 18 May 1827. In the early days of the Republic, as today, a display of naval might brought a nation prestige and enhanced her commerce. Such was the case with Rodgers' squadron, which laid the groundwork for the 1830 commercial treaty with Turkey which opened ports of the Eastern Mediterranean and the Black Sea to American traders.

Figure 22 - USS North Carolina at anchor, NARA

After a period in ordinary at Norfolk, *North Carolina* was decommissioned 30 October 1836 to fit out for the Pacific Station, the one other area where ships of her vast size could be employed. Only the Mediterranean and the western coast of South America had ports that could accommodate ships of great draft. Once again flagship of her station, *North Carolina* reached Callao, Peru, 26 May 1837. With war raging between Chile and Peru, and relations between the United States and Mexico strained, *North Carolina* protected the important American commerce of the eastern Pacific until March 1839. Since her great size made her less flexible than smaller ships, she returned to the New York Navy Yard in June, and served as a receiving ship until placed in ordinary in 1866. She was sold at New York 1 October 1867 for $30,000. The figurehead of the ship, a bust of Sir Walter Raleigh was given to the state of North Carolina in 1909.

Ohio

Ohio was admitted to the Union 1 March 1803 as the 17th State.

L/B/D: 208'; b. 53'10"; d. 26'0"
Tons: 2,724
Comp.: 840
Arm.: 74 32pdr (as authorized)
      86-102 32-42pdr long guns, 32pdr, later 42pdr carr. (operational)
Des.: Designer: Eckford, builder: New York Navy Yard
Laid down: 1817
Launched: 30 May 1820
Commissioned: September 1838
Disposition: Sold at Boston to J. L. Snow of Rockland, Maine 27 September 1883. She was burned to recover her fittings in the following year, in Greenpoint Harbor, New York

Figure 23 - USS Ohio-Lithograph, hand colored by N. Currier, 152 Nassau Street, N.Y.

Ohio was long considered the one of the finest vessels of her rate in the world, if not the finest, and by far the best liner in the American Navy. Not only was she a handsome ship of her type, but also she was a remarkable sailor and a good sea boat, carrying her guns high, and stowed her allowances with ease. It was often said she handled like a frigate.

The armament of *Ohio* varied from time to time. When she was built, the liner was armed in what was then considered an effective way: all guns of the same caliber, 32pdrs, the long guns on the lower deck being somewhat heavier then those of the main. Later the lower deck was armed with long 42pdrs the carronades also became 42pdrs. The total numbers of guns varied with each commander, ranging from 86 to 102.

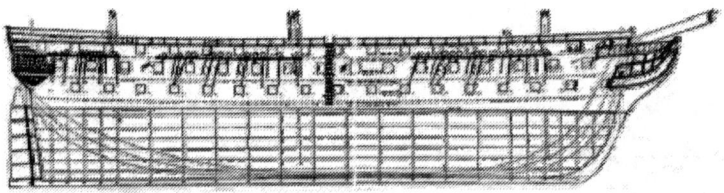

Figure 24 - Draught of the 74-gun ship Ohio

She went into ordinary after she was launched and in the ensuing years decayed badly. Refitted for service in 1838, *Ohio* sailed 16 October 1838 to join the Mediterranean Squadron under Commodore Issac Hull. Acting as flagship for 2 years, she protected commerce and suppressed the slave trade off the African coast. *Ohio* proved to be an excellent sailor repeatedly making more than 12 knots. One of her officers stated, *"I never supposed such a ship could be built-a ship possessing in so great a degree all the qualifications of a perfect vessel."* In 1840 *Ohio* returned to Boston where she again went into ordinary. From 1841 to 1846 *Ohio* served as receiving ship. Quarter Master Frederick Boyer, subject of one of the earliest known portraits of a U.S. Navy enlisted man, served in the *Ohio* while she was receiving ship at the Boston Navy Yard during the early 1840s. A contemporary described him as having had "Twenty years in the Navy".

Figure 25 - Quarter Master Frederick Boyer Oil on canvas, 29" x 24", by Henry C. Flagg Painted circa 1840-1845.

To meet the needs of the Mexican War, *Ohio* recommissioned 7 December 1846 and sailed 4 January 1847 for the Gulf of Mexico, arriving off Vera Cruz 22 March. *Ohio* landed 10 guns on 27 March to help in the siege of Vera Cruz; but the city soon surrendered.

Ohio drew too much water for coastal operations in the gulf, however, 336 of her crew participated in the Tuxpan River Expedition. In 1847 the entire distance from the mouth of the river to the town was covered with thick jungle growth. The enemy had constructed three well-positioned forts on bluffs overlooking bends in the river. On 18 April, Commodore Perry arrived off the mouth of the river with 15 vessels. At 10 p.m. light-draft steamers *Scourge*, *Spitfire*, and *Vixen*, each towing a schooner, moved up stream. Bomb ships, *Etna*, *Hecla*, and *Vesuvius* followed closely while 30 surf boats containing 1,500 men brought up the rear. Approaching the town, the squadron came under hot fire from Fort LaPena. Commodore Matthew C. Perry ordered Commander Franklin Buchanan to disembark the surfboats and storm the fort. As the landing party swept ashore, the Mexicans abandoned their position. The other two forts fell in a like manner, with only light casualties sustained by the squadron. Men from *Ohio* retrieved the guns of brig *Truxtun* that had foundered in a storm near Tuxpan 16 September 1846. The town was occupied and all military stores destroyed.

Following Tuxpan, *Ohio* sailed from Vera Cruz and arrived in New York 9 May 1847. On 26 June, she sailed to bolster the Pacific Squadron, first carrying the

U.S. minister to Brazil and operating off the east coast of South America until November. *Ohio* spent the next two years in the Pacific protecting commerce and policing the newly acquired California Territory during the chaotic early months of the gold rush.

Figure 26 - USS Ohio, Boston, Mass 1850s, NARA

In 1850, she returned to Boston where she again went into ordinary. In 1851 *Ohio* became receiving ship and continued this duty until again placed in ordinary in 1875. *Ohio* was sold at Boston to J. L. Snow of Rockland, Maine 27 September 1883. She was burned in the following year, in Greenpoint Harbor, New York; the remains are still accessible to scuba divers.

Overlooking Stony Brook Harbor, the Hercules Pavilion on Main Street, Stony Brook, houses the figurehead and anchor from the *Ohio*, The figurehead, depicting Hercules wrapped in the skin of the Nemean Lion was carved from a single piece of cedar at a cost of $1,500.

Figure 27 - Figurehead of USS Ohio, The Ward Melville Heritage Organization.

The massive bust was first sold for $10 to the Aldrich family of Aquebogue; then to Miles Carpenter, owner of the Canoe Place Inn in Hampton Bays, for $15. Near the turn of the century, a legend was inscribed on the figurehead's pedestal stating that any maiden who kissed the forehead of the mighty Hercules would be wed within a year. The Canoe Place Inn site overlooking the Shinnecock Canal was home to Hercules for decades. Subsequently the figurehead was acquired by philanthropist Ward Melville who deeded it to The Ward Melville Heritage Organization for preservation.

Pennsylvania

Pennsylvania, second of the original 13 states, ratified the Constitution 12 December 1787.

L/B/D: 210'0"; b. 56'9"; d. 24'4" (dpth of hold)
Tons: 3,105
Comp.: 1,100
Arm.: 74 32pdr (as authorized)
Pierced for 132 exclusive of bow/stern chasers(as built)
1842 survey: 12x8" shell guns, 90x32pdr
Des.: Designer: Samuel Humphreys, builder: Philadelphia Navy Yard
Laid down: September 1821
Launched: 18 July 1837
Commissioned: 30 November 1837
Disposition: Burned to the waterline to prevent her falling into Confederate hands, 20 April 1861, Norfolk Navy Yard.

Figure 28 - USS Pennsylvania-Lithograph, hand colored by N. Currier, 152 Nassau Street, N.Y.

Ship-of-the-line *Pennsylvania* was one of "nine ships to rate not less than 74 guns each" authorized by Congress 29 April 1816. She was designed and built by Samuel Humphreys in the Philadelphia Navy Yard. Her keel was laid in

September 1821, but tight budgets slowed her construction, preventing her being launched until 18 July 1837. The largest sailing warship ever built for the U.S. Navy, she had four complete gun decks of which three were covered and no poop deck. Her hull was pierced for 132 guns exclusive of bow chases and stern guns.

Initially, she was to have had a small beak head bulkhead, but as the design developed over eight years, this was dropped in favor of a rounded bow. The work on this massive ship occupied the Philadelphia Navy Yard carpenters to such an extent that little other work was done while she was building.

Figure 29 - Building draught for the 120-gun ship Pennsylvania, showing ship as launched and fitted

Her design pointed to a ship capable of breaking a blockade, rather then leading a cruising squadron, nevertheless, she could perform either service is necessary. She had no pretension of grace, being merely a powerful gun carrier of enormous displacement for her length, Humphreys, recognizing her short comings, altered her run late in the design in an effort to improve her sailing qualities with limited success, she was know through out the fleet as a cumbersome "crank" and not very weatherly. To be fair, commanders trained in smart frigates and handy 74's such as *Columbus*, *Franklin*, *Ohio*, and the ever-popular *North Carolina* would find her to be a handful and a poor sailor. Her high freeboard and full lines would have prevented her from sailing as fast as the *Ohio*.

Do to the expense of manning her; she saw little active service and her sailing capabilities were never fully explored. In fact, the cost of maintaining her was the greatest objection to keeping her in service, a statement that could be applied to the entire class of liners in peacetime.

Exploding shell guns were replacing solid shot by the time *Pennsylvania* was fitting out. A Bureau of Ordnance gun register for 1846 records her armament as follows: Spar deck: two nine-pounder cannons and one small brass swivel. Main deck: four 8-inch chambered cannons received from Norfolk in 1842, and thirty-two 32-pounder cannons. Middle deck: four 8-inch chambered cannons received from Norfolk in 1842, and thirty 32-pounder cannons. Lower deck: four 8-inch chambered cannons and twenty-eight 32-pounder cannons.

Shifting from her launching site to off Chester, Pa., 29 November 1837, she was partially manned there the following day. Only 34 of her guns were noted as having been mounted 3 December 1837. She stood downriver for Newcastle, Del., 9 December, to receive gun carriages and other equipage before proceeding to the Norfolk Navy Yard for coppering her hull. She departed Newcastle 20 December 1837 and discharged the Delaware pilot on the 25th. That afternoon she sailed for the Virginia Capes. She came off the Norfolk dry dock 2 January 1838. That day her crew transferred to *Columbia*.

Figure 30 - Destruction of Norfolk Navy Yard 20 April 1861. *Detail of Photo# NH 59179*

Pennsylvania remained in ordinary until 1842 when she became a receiving ship for the Norfolk Navy Yard. She remained in the Yard until 20 April 1861 when she was burned to the waterline to prevent her falling into Confederate hands.

Vermont

Vermont, the 14th state, was admitted to the Union on 4 March 1791

L/B/D: 196'3"; b. 53'6"; d. 26'2"
Tons: 2,633
Comp.: 820 (designed)
339 (1863 store ship)
Arm.: 74 32pdr (as authorized)
16 guns (as stores ship)
Des.: Designer: Doughty, builder: Boston Navy Yard
Laid down: September 1818
Launched: 15 September 1848
Commissioned: 30 January 1862
Disposition: Struck from the Navy list on 19 December 1901 and was sold at New York on 17 April 1902.

Figure 31 - Period etching of USS Vermont at anchor

The first *Vermont* was one of nine 74-gun warships authorized by Congress on 29 April 1816. She was laid down at the Boston Navy Yard in September 1818; finished about 1825; and kept on the stocks until finally launched at Boston on 15 September 1848 in the interest of both space and fire safety considerations.

Like her near sister *New Hampshire*, she originally was to have the curved upper head rails popular at the start of the War of 1812. However, the straight rails introduced into the Royal Navy much earlier as a matter of wartime economy were installed on all ships of the line after 1820.

Designed to be an improvement on the wartime liners, these ships were in fact only slightly improved over *Columbus*, the best of the previous class. Being fast sailors and of stronger construction, they were deemed acceptable and the design was not altered.

However, *Vermont* was not commissioned at this time. Instead, the already aged ship of the line remained in ordinary at Boston until the outbreak of the Civil War in April 1861. The cavernous hull of the vessel was badly needed as a store and receiving ship at Port Royal, S.C. and she was commissioned at Boston on 30 January 1862, Comdr. Augustus S. Baldwin in command. She received orders to sail for Port Royal for duty with Rear Admiral Samuel F. Du Pont's South Atlantic Blockading Squadron on 17 February and left Boston on 24 February under tow by the steamer Kensington.

That evening, a violent northwest gale accompanied by snow struck the vessels while off Cape Cod Light, Mass. Kensington let go the towlines, but *Vermont* refused to obey her helm, broached, and had all her sails and most of her boats blown and torn away. The gale raged for fifty hours and by the morning of the 26th, *Vermont* was drifting eastward with no rudder, her berth deck flooded, and much of the interior of the vessel destroyed. Later on the 26th, *Vermont* sighted the schooner *Flying Mist*, hailed her, put a man on board and persuaded her captain to return to the east coast and report the helpless condition of the ship to naval authorities. Rescue vessels began to reach the stricken warship on 7 March and enabled *Vermont* to sail into Port Royal under her own power on 12 April. *Vermont* remained anchored at Port Royal where she served the South Atlantic Blockading Squadron as ordnance, hospital, receiving, and store ship drawing praise from Rear Admiral Du Pont.

Figure 32 - USS Vermont Group of contrabands From U S Navy Edisto Island. Morris and Folly Islands Fort Warren Mass Andersonville Prison Miscellaneous photographic album p 50

A great many of *Vermont's* crew during this period were *contrabands*, freed slaves who served in many capacities in Union forces during the war. An Extract from the work of researcher Constance V. Brooks shows *Vermont* on July 1, 1863 with a contraband roll noting 143 sailors, all rated as landsmen. The previous muster roll, dated March 31, 1863, does not separate contrabands from the rest of the crew. "Negro" William Johnson, a Virginia-born barber who enlisted in Boston, appears on this muster roll and on subsequent rolls for *Vermont's* crew members counted as free when enlisting.

TOTAL RECAPITULATION FOR THE CREW ON MARCH 31, 1863:
Petty Officers, 31;
Seamen, 20; Ordinary Seamen, 12; Landsmen, 39;
Boys, 9; Marines, 47; Contrabands, 175, Coal heavers, 6.
Total in crew: 339

Figure 33 - USS Vermont Deck view From U S Navy Edisto Island. Morris and Folly Islands Fort Warren Mass Andersonville Prison Miscellaneous photographic album p 50

The Navy had been from its very beginning somewhat racially integrated when viewed from the separation of the races that was the norm in American society. Auxiliary ships tended to have a higher proportion of blacks on their muster rolls, reflecting the need for a larger number of unskilled labor needed for work not related to handling the ship or her guns.

Secretary of the Navy Gideon Welles ordered the vessel to return to New York for "public service" on 25 July 1864. She left Port Royal on 2 August and was replaced there by her sister ship-of-the-line *New Hampshire.*

Figure 34 - Vermont as a receiving ship, New York Navy Yard. NARA

Vermont, her masts removed and decked over, remained at New York for the next 37 years, serving both as a store and receiving ship. She was condemned and struck from the Navy list on 19 December 1901 and was sold at New York on 17 April 1902.

Virginia

The first English colony in America and one of the original 13 states.

L/B/D: 196'3"; b. 54'4"; d. 26'2"
Tons: 2,633 (designed)
Comp.: 820 (designed)
Arm.: 74 32pdr (designed)
Des.: Designer: Doughty, builder: Boston Navy Yard
Laid down: May 1822
Launched: Never
Commissioned: Never
Disposition: Broken up on the stocks 1874

Virginia was one of "nine ships to rate not less than 74 guns each" authorized by Congress 29 April 1816. Her keel was laid May 1822 in the Boston Navy Yard and she was largely complete by 1825. For economy, she was preserved on the stocks to be launched should national interests require. She remained on the stocks until broken up in 1874. Her design tonnage was 2,633.

Washington

George Washington, General and first President of the United States.

L/B/D: 190'2"; b. 55'4"; dph. 19'9"; dr. 24'4"
Tons: 2,250
Comp.: 820
Arm.: 74 32pdr
Des.: Designer: Portsmouth (N.H.) Navy Yard under a contract with the shipbuilders, Hartt and Badger
Laid down: May 1813
Launched: 1 October 1814
Commissioned: 26 August 1815
Disposition: Broken up at New York 1843

Figure 35 - Primitive painting of USS Washington at anchor.

The fourth *Washington*-a 74-gun ship-of-the-line- was authorized by Congress on 2 January 1813 and was laid down in May of that year at the Portsmouth (N.H.) Navy Yard under a contract with the shipbuilders, Hartt and Badger. The ship was launched on 1 October 1814 and was commissioned at Portsmouth on 26 August 1815, Capt. John O. Creighton in command.

As designed, her appearance was similar to the 1799 74-gun ship design of Joshua Humphreys, however she was 4 feet longer and no longer sported the rounded bow of those proposed ships. She, like *Columbus, Franklin* and *Independence* suffered from being over gunned for their displacement. Do to the prevailing Navy Board thinking, her ordinance was not reduced to allow her to show more height above the water line.

Figure 36 - The launching of USS Washington Portsmouth Navy Yard, NH 1 Oct 1814. NARA

After fitting out, *Washington* sailed for Boston on 3 December 1815. In the spring of the following year, the ship-of-the-line shifted to Annapolis, Md., and arrived there on 15 May 1816. Over the ensuing days, the man-of-war welcomed a number of distinguished visitors who came on board to inspect what was, in those days, one of the more powerful ships afloat. The guests included Commodore John Rodgers and Capt. David Porter; Col. Franklin Wharton, the Commandant of the Marine Corps; and President and Mrs. James Madison. The Chief Executive and his lady came on board *"at half past meridian, to visit the ship, on which occasion yards were manned and they were saluted with 19 guns and three cheers."*

Washington then sailed down Chesapeake Bay and embarked William Pinckney and his "suite" on 5 June. On 8 June, the ship of the line set sail for the Mediterranean flying the broad pennant of Commodore Isaac Chauncey, the commander of the fledgling United States Navy's Mediterranean Squadron. *Washington* reached Gibraltar on 2 July, in route to her ultimate destination, Naples.
Washington made port at Naples on 25 July, and Pickney debarked to commence his special mission- to adjust the claims of American merchants against the Neapolitan authorities. The talks ensued well into August. At the end of the month, the demands of diplomacy apparently satisfied, *Washington* set sail.

For the next two years, the ship-of-the-line operated in the Mediterranean as flagship of the American squadron. She provided a display of force to encourage the Barbary States to respect American commerce. Dignitaries that visited the American man-of-war during this Mediterranean cruise included General Nugent, the commander in chief of Austrian forces (on 5 August 1817) and Prince Henry of Prussia (on 12 August 1817). On 1 February 1818, Commodore Charles Stewart relieved Commodore Chauncey as commander of the American Mediterranean Squadron at Syracuse harbor, after which time *Washington* cruised to Messina and the Barbary Coast. She set sail for home on 23 May 1818-convoying 40 American merchantmen-and reached New York on 6 July 1818. The next day, the Vice President of the United States, Daniel D. Tompkins, visited the ship; and the warship blocked her colors at half-mast on the 8th, in honor of the interment of the remains of General Richard Montgomery, who had been killed leading the Continental assault against Quebec in 1775.

Washington did little cruising thereafter, remaining at New York as Commodore Chauncey's flagship until 1820. Placed "in ordinary" that year, the ship-of-the-line remained inactive until 1843. Do to her hasty construction with green timber, and her long period of inactive service-when the money to be used for her maintenance diverted to other needs of the navy, she was deemed rotted beyond repair and broken up.

Tables

Table 1 Summary of Service

Name	Authorized	Laid Down	Launched	Commissioned	Disposed of
America	20 November 1776	May 1777	5 Nov 1782	Never	June 1783, transferred to France
Chippewa	3 March 1813	January 1815	Never	Never	1 Nov 1833, broken up
Columbus	2 January 1813[1]	June 1816	1 March 1819	7 September 1819	20 April 1861, burned by Federal forces, Norfolk Navy Yard
Delaware	29 April 1816	August 1817	21 October 1820	27 March 1827	20 April 1861, burned by Federal forces, Norfolk Navy Yard
Franklin	2 January 1813	May 1813	August 1815	October 1815	1852, broken up, Portsmouth, NH
Independence[2]	2 January 1813	May 1813	22 June 1814	July 1814	20 September 1919, burned, San Francisco, Ca.
New Hampshire	29 April 1816	June 1819	23 April 1864	13 May 1864[3]	July 26 1922, burned under tow, Massachusetts Bay
New Orleans	3 March 1813	January 1815	Never	Never	24 September 1883, broken up, Sacketts Harbor, N.Y.
New York	29 April 1816	1820	Never	Never	20 April 1861, burned by Federal forces, Norfolk Navy Yard
North Carolina	29 April 1816	1818	7 September 1820	24 June 1824	1 October 1867, broken up, New York, N.Y.
Ohio	29 April 1816	1817	30 May 1820	September 1838	September 1884, burned, Greenpoint Harbor, N.Y.
Pennsylvania	29 April 1816	1822	18 July 1837	30 November 1837	20 April 1861, burned by Federal forces, Norfolk Navy Yard
Vermont	29 April 1816	September 1818	15 September 1848	April 1861[4]	17 April 1902, sold, broken up, New York, N.Y.
Virginia	29 April 1816	May 1822	Never	Never	1874, broken up, Boston, Mass.
Washington	2 January 1813	May 1813	1 October 1814	26 August 1815	1843, broken up, New York, N.Y

[1] Her construction was delayed, reauthorized 29 April 1816.
[2] Razeed to a 54-gun frigate in 1836.
[3] Commissioned as a stores ship in support of the Federal Blockade of the Confederate States of America.
[4] Commissioned as a stores ship in support of the Federal Blockade of the Confederate States of America.

Table 2 Comparison of the ships of the line						
Name	Length	Beam	Depth	Tons	Comp	Guns
America	182'6"[5]	50'6"	23'	1,982	626	(74) 66
Chippewa	204'	56'	??	2,805	??	74-130[6]
Columbus	193' 3"	52'0"	21' 10"	2,480	780	(74) 92
Delaware	196'3"	54'4"	26'2"	2,633	820	74
Franklin	187' 10 ¾"	50'0"	19'9"	2,257	820	(74) 87
Independence	190'10"	54'7"	21'4"	2,243	790	(74) 87
New Hampshire	196'3"	53'6"	21' 6"	2,633	340	(74) 10[7]
New Orleans	204'0"	56'	26'0"	2,805	??	(74) 130
New York	196'3"	54'4"	26'2"	2,633	820	74
North Carolina	196'3"	53'6"	26'2"	2,633	820	(74) 94
Ohio	208'0"	53'10"	26'0"	2,724	840	(74) 86-102
Pennsylvania	210'0"	56'9"	24'4"	3,105	1,100	(120) 132
Vermont	196'3"	53'6"	26'2"	2,633	339	(74) 16[8]
Virginia	196'3"	54'4"	26'2"	2,633	820	74
Washington	190'2	55'4	19'9"	2,250	820	74
HMS Asia[9]	196'1"	51"1	22"5"	2898	700	84

---

[1] Gun deck length

[6] Design up gunned during construction to counter Royal Navy ships of the line being constructed on Lake Ontario.

[7] As a stores ship

[8] As a stores ship

[9] HMS Asia -added as a reference to a well-known European ship of the line, launched in 1824 at Bombay India. Built of Teak, rather then oak, she also incorporated Sir Robert Seppings hull construction techniques. She was active until 1852, broken up in 1906.

Table 3 Chronology of events

1776
9 November
The Continental Congress authorized the construction of three 74-gun ships of the line. Only *America* was ever constructed.

1777
May
America laid down at Rising Castle (now Badger) Island in the Piscataqua River between Portsmouth, N.H., and Kittery, Maine.

1778
29th May
The Marine Committee reported in favor of making *America* a razee two-decker.

1779
6 November
The Marine Committee named Capt. John Barry as *America's* prospective commanding officer. Capt. Berry convinces the Marine Committee not to razee *America*.

1780
5 September
Captain Berry ordered to Boston to take command of the 36-gun frigate *Alliance*.

1781
23 June
The Continental Congress ordered the Continental Agent of Marine, Robert Morris, to get *America* ready for sea.
26 June
Capt. John Paul Jones assigned as *America's* commanding officer.
31 August
Jones reached Portsmouth.

1782
11 August
French ship of the line *Magnifique* runs aground and is destroyed while attempting to enter Boston harbor.
3 September
The Continental Congress decides to present *America* to King Louis XVI of France to replace the French ship of the line *Magnifique*.
5 November
America launched.

1783
24 June

Chevalier de Macarty Martinge, who had commanded *Magnifique* when she was wrecked-departs Portsmouth, NH in command of *L' Amerique (America)*.
16 July
L' Amerique reaches Brest, France.
3 September
Signing of Treaty of Paris ends American Revolution.

1786
L' Amerique, surveyed and found to be badly rotted, is broken up.
1794
27 March
Congress authorizes construction of six frigates.
5 June
First officers of the U.S. Navy under the Constitution are appointed.
1797
Secretary of the Navy Stoddert suggests to congress the need for twelve 74-gun ships of the line.
1 July
Naval Regulations passed by Congress.
1798
11 July Reestablishment of the Marine Corps under the Constitution.

1799
Congress authorizes the purchase of six sets of frames for 74-gun ships.
20 March
Joshua Humpherys completes initial draught for the "Independence class" 74-gun ships. None were ever constructed.
1812
18 June
U.S. declares war on Great Britain for impressments of sailors and interference with commerce.

1813
2 January
Columbus, Franklin, Independence & Washington authorized.
3 March
Chippewa & New Orleans authorized.
May
Independence, Franklin & Washington laid down

1814
22 June

Independence launched at Boston.
July
Independence commissioned.
1 October
Washington launched at Portsmouth (N.H.) Navy Yard.
24 December
Treaty of Ghent, British and American diplomats agreed on status quo ante bellum

1815
3 July
Independence, Captain William Crane commanding, departs for the Mediterranean as Commodore William Bainbridge's flagship.
August
Franklin launched at Philadelphia Navy Yard.
January
Chippewa laid down Sacketts Harbor, N.Y., ready for launch 42 days later.
New Orleans laid down at Sacketts Harbor, N.Y.
17 February
President Madison signed the American ratification of the Treaty of Ghent, and the treaty was proclaimed the following day.
March
Chippewa housed over, still on the stocks.
April
New Orleans, ready for launch is housed over on the stocks.
26 August
Washington commissioned at Portsmouth (N.H.) Navy Yard
October
Franklin commissioned at Philadelphia Navy Yard.
15 November
Independence arrives at Boston from Mediterranean deployment.
3 December
Washington sails for Boston.

1816
29 April
Delaware, New Hampshire, New York, North Carolina, Ohio, Pennsylvania, Vermont, Virginia authorized; *Columbus* reauthorized.
15 May
Washington arrives at Annapolis, Md.
8 June,
Washington departs Annapolis, Md. for the Mediterranean flying the broad pennant of Commodore Isaac Chauncey, the commander of the fledgling United States Navy's Mediterranean Squadron.

June
Columbus laid down.
2 July
Washington reached Gibraltar.
25 July
Washington makes port at Naples, Italy.

1817
Washington cruises in the Mediterranean.
Delaware Laid down Norfolk Navy Yard.
Ohio laid down at New York Navy Yard.
April
Doughty recommended do to her obvious faults, *Independence* be razeed to a frigate.
14 October
Franklin departs from Philadelphia under the command of Master Commandant H.E. Ballard. She carried the Hon. Richard Rush, U.S. Minister to England, to his post. Subsequently she was designated flagship of the Mediterranean Squadron.

1818
North Carolina laid down at Philadelphia Navy Yard.
23 May
Washington departs the Mediterranean in route New York.
6 July
Washington arrives at New York, assigned to the Home Squadron.
September
Vermont laid down at Boston Navy Yard.

1819
1 March
Columbus launched.
June
Alabama (*New Hampshire*) laid down.
7 September
Columbus commissioned.
29 November
Commodore John Shaw relieves Commodore Bainbridge at Boston; *Independence* remains the flagship of the squadron based there.

1820
Washington placed in ordinary at New York.
New York laid down at Norfolk Navy Yard.
28 April

Columbus departs Norfolk, Va., serves as flagship for Commodore W. Bainbridge in the Mediterranean until returning to Boston.
30 May
Ohio launched at New York Navy Yard. She went into ordinary after she was launched and in the ensuing years decayed badly.
7 September
North Carolina launched at Philadelphia Navy Yard.
21 October
Delaware launched. Roofed over, she is kept at the Norfolk Navy Yard in ordinary.
March
Franklin departs the Mediterranean.
24 April
Franklin arrives at New York Navy Yard.

1821
23 July 1821
Columbus returns to Boston from Mediterranean deployment.
September
Pennsylvania laid down at Philadelphia Navy Yard.

1822
Independence placed in ordinary at Boston.
Virginia laid down at Boston Navy Yard.

1827
27 March
Delaware commissioned

1828
10 February
Delaware, under the command of Captain J. Downs departs for the Mediterranean to become the flagship of Commodore W. I. M. Crane.
23 March
Delaware Arrives at Algeciras Bay, Spain
11 October
Franklin assumes duties as flagship on the Pacific Station.

1824
24 June
North Carolina commissioned at Philadelphia Navy Yard. Master Commandant Charles W. Morgan assigned to *North Carolina* as her first commanding officer.
29 August
Franklin relinquishes duties as flagship on the Pacific Station.

1825

Virginia ready for launch-remains on the stocks as an economy measure.
Alabama (*New Hampshire*) ready for launch, remains on the stocks as an economy measure.
29 April
North Carolina in the Mediterranean as flagship for Commodore John Rodgers.

1827
18 May
North Carolina relinquishes duties as the Mediterranean squadron flagship. Assigned to the Home Squadron.

1830
2 January
Delaware arrives at Norfolk, Virginia.
10 February
Delaware is placed in ordinary at Norfolk.

1833
15 July
Delaware is recommissioned at Norfolk, Virginia.
29 July
Delaware receives President Jackson on board, firing a 24-gun salute at both his arrival and departure.
30 July
Delaware deploys for the Mediterranean where she served as flagship for Commodore D. T. Patterson.
1 November
Chippewa still on the stocks, sold for scrapping.
Columbus placed in ordinary as a receiving ship, Boston

1836
Independence placed in Boston Navy Yard dry dock #1 and razeed. She is rated down to a 54-gun frigate.
16 February
Delaware arrives Norfolk, Virginia form Mediterranean deployment.
10 March
Delaware placed in ordinary, Norfolk, Virginia.
30 October
North Carolina decommissioned to fit out for the Pacific Station.

1837
26 March
Independence is recommissioned at Boston as a 54-gun frigate.
20 May
Independence sails from Boston as flagship of Commodore John B. Nicholson in route Kronstadt, Russia.

26 May
Again flagship of her station, *North Carolina* reached Callao, Peru.
13 June
Independence arrives at Portsmouth, England.
18 July
Pennsylvania launched at the Philadelphia Navy Yard.
29 July
Independence arrives at Kronstadt to receive a visit from the Emperor of Russia. Two days later, a steamboat arrived to transport Honorable George Dallas, Minister to Russia and his family to St. Petersburg.
13 August
Independence departs Kronstadt for Rio de Janeiro.
September
Independence becomes flagship of the Brazil Squadron.
30 November
Pennsylvania commissioned at the Philadelphia Navy Yard
26 December
Pennsylvania arrives at Norfolk Navy Yard.

1838
January
Pennsylvania placed in ordinary at Norfolk Navy Yard.
September
Ohio commissioned at New York Navy Yard.
16 October
Ohio departs New York to join the Mediterranean Squadron under Commodore Issac Hull. She Acts as flagship for 2 years.

1839
March
North Carolina departs the eastern Pacific in route New York
June
North Carolina converted to a receiving ship, New York Navy Yard.

1840
Ohio returns to Boston and is placed in ordinary.
30 March
Independence returns to New York and is laid up in ordinary.

1841
Ohio converted to a receiving ship at Boston Navy Yard.
7 May
Delaware recommissioned at Norfolk, Virginia.
1 November

Delaware sails for a tour of duty on the Brazil Station as flagship for Commodore C. Morris.

1842
Pennsylvania converted to a receiving ship at Norfolk Navy Yard
14 May
Independence becomes flagship of Commodore Charles Stewart in the Home Squadron
29 August
Columbus deploys to the Mediterranean as flagship for Commodore C. W. Morgan.

1843
Washington surveyed and is determined to be beyond economic repair-broken up at New York.
19 February
Delaware sails from Rio de Janeiro for the Mediterranean.
24 February
Columbus sails from Genoa, Italy, in route Rio de Janeiro, Brazil.
29 July
Columbus becomes flagship of the Brazil Squadron, Commodore D. Turner.
Franklin ordered to Boston as a receiving ship.

1844
4 March
Delaware arrives at Norfolk, Virginia from the Mediterranean.
22 March
Delaware placed in ordinary at Norfolk Navy Yard.
27 May
Columbus returns to New York for repairs.

1845
4 June
Columbus embarks Commodore J. Biddle, Commander East Indies Squadron, and sails for Canton, China.
3 December
Independence laid up in ordinary.
31 December
Commodore Biddle, on board *Columbus*, exchanges ratified copies of the first American commercial treaty with China.

1846
April
Columbus departs Canton, China.
April 25
The first battle between the Mexican and U.S. armies.

19 July
Columbus, in company with *Vincennes*, arrives at Tokyo Bay in an attempt opening Japan to American commerce.
4 August
Independence recommissioned.
29 August
Independence departs Boston for California.
7 December
Ohio recommissioned to provide support for the Mexican-American War.

1847
4 January
Ohio departs Boston for the Gulf of Mexico.
22 January
Independence enters Monterey Bay and became the flagship of Commodore William B. Shubrick, commanding the Pacific Squadron.
2 March
Columbus arrives off Monterey, California.
22 March
Ohio arrives off Vera Cruz.
27 March
Ohio landed 10 guns to help in the siege of Vera Cruz.
9 May
Ohio arrives at New York from Vera Cruz.
16 May
Independence captures Mexican ship *Correo* and a launch.
26 June
Ohio departs New York for the Pacific Station.
25 July
Columbus departs San Francisco, California.
19 October
Independence supports the capture of Guaymas.
11 November
Independence lands blue jackets and Marines to occupy Mazatlan.
December
Recalled at the outbreak of the Mexican War *Columbus* reached Valparaiso, Chile.

1848
Ohio cruises the Pacific protecting commerce and policing the newly acquired California Territory.
February 2
The signing of the Treaty of Guadeloupe Hidalgo, the Mexican-American war ends.

3 March
Columbus arrives at Norfolk, Virginia and is placed in ordinary.
12 August
Independence arrives at Honolulu.
15 September
Vermont launched at Boston Navy Yard, placed in ordinary.

1849
Ohio cruises the Pacific protecting commerce and policing the newly acquired California Territory.
23 May
Independence returns to Norfolk, Virginia, after extensive cruising in the Eastern Pacific.
30 May
Independence is decommissioned at Norfolk, Virginia.
7 July
Independence recommissioned at Norfolk, Virginia.
26 July
Independence departs Norfolk, Virginia under Captain Thomas A. Conover to serve as flagship of the Mediterranean Squadron under Commodore Charles W. Morgan.

1850
Ohio returns to Boston where she goes into ordinary.
23 May
Independence arrives Spezia, Italy, She is the first U.S. man-of-war to show the flag at that port.

1851
Ohio is converted to a receiving ship at Boston Navy Yard.

1852
Franklin broken up at Portsmouth, NH.
25 June
Independence Returns to Norfolk, Virginia.
3 July
Independence placed in ordinary at New York.

1854
September
Independence is recommissioned at New York Navy Yard.
10 October
Independence departs New York to serve as flagship of the Pacific Squadron under Commodore William Mervine.

1855
2 February

Independence arrives at Valparaiso, Chile.
Independence cruises extensively in the Eastern Pacific.

1856
Independence cruises extensively in the Eastern Pacific.

1857
Independence cruises extensively in the Eastern Pacific.
2 October
Independence enters the Mare Island Navy Yard; she is converted to a receiving ship.

1860
December 20
South Carolina becomes first state to secede from the United States of America.

1861
4 February
The Confederate States of America is formed.
17 April
Virginia secedes from the Union.
20 April
Columbus, Delaware, New York, Pennsylvania destroyed at Norfolk Navy Yard by withdrawing Union forces to prevent them falling into Confederate hands
28 October
Alabama renamed *New Hampshire*.

1862
30 January
Vermont commissioned at Boston Navy Yard as a stores ship.
24 February
Under tow by the steamer Kensington, *Vermont* departs for Port Royal, South Carolina assigned to Rear Admiral Samuel F. Du Font's South Atlantic Blockading Squadron
25 February
Vermont cast a drift in a gale off Cape Cod Light, Mass.
7 March
Rescue ships reach the disabled *Vermont*.
12 April
Vermont sails into Port Royal, South Carolina under her own power.

1864
23 April 1864
New Hampshire launched.
13 May
New Hampshire commissioned as a stores ship.

15 June
New Hampshire sails from Portsmouth in route South Atlantic Blockading Squadron.
25 July
Secretary of the Navy Gideon Welles orders *Vermont* to return to New York for "public service".
29 July
New Hampshire assumes duties as store and depot ship at Port Royal, South Carolina, serving there through the end of the Civil War.
2 August
Vermont departs Port Royal, South Carolina for New York.
September
Vermont assumes duties as both a store and receiving ship at New York.

1865
June
All Confederate lands forces have surrendered to the United States.
November
All Confederate naval forces have surrendered.

1866
North Carolina placed in ordinary at New York Navy Yard.
8 June
New Hampshire arrives at Norfolk, Virginia.

1867
1 October
North Carolina Sold at New York for $30,000 and broken up.

1874
Virginia broken up, still on the stocks.

1875
Ohio placed in ordinary at Boston Navy Yard.

1876
10 May
New Hampshire arrives at Port Royal, South Carolina.

1881
New Hampshire returns to Norfolk, Virginia-but soon shifts to Newport, Rhode Island. She becomes flagship of Commodore Stephen B. Luce's newly formed Apprentice Training Squadron.

1883
24 September

New Orleans sold to H. Wilkinson, Jr., of Syracuse, N.Y., broken up on the stocks.
27 September
Ohio sold at Boston to J. L. Snow of Rockland, Maine.

1884
Ohio burned to recover her fittings in Greenpoint Harbor, New York

1891
New Hampshire is towed from Newport to New London, Connecticut, and is used as a receiving ship.

1892
5 June
New Hampshire is decommissioned.

1893
New Hampshire is loaned as training ship for the New York State Naval Militia. Stationed in the Hudson River.

1898
15 February
USS *Maine* a second-class armored battleship-explodes at anchor in Havana harbor, Cuba.
21 April to 13 August
The Spanish-American War, the New York State Naval Militia furnishes nearly a thousand officers and men who had been trained on *New Hampshire*.

1901
19 December
Vermont stricken from the Navy List.

1902
17 April
Vermont sold for scraping at New York.

1904
30 November
New Hampshire is renamed *Granite State* to free the name "New Hampshire" for a newly authorized battleship (BB-25).

1909
The figurehead of the *North Carolina*, a bust of Sir Walter Raleigh is given to the state of North Carolina.

1912
3 November
Independence is decommissioned.

1913
3 September
Independence is struck from the Navy List.

1914
28 June
Emperor Franz Joseph of Austria-Hungary declares war on Serbia, igniting World War I.
28 November
Independence is towed to Union Iron Works, San Francisco

1915
5 March
Independence is moved to Hunter's Point.

1917
6 April
President Wilson asks Congress for a declaration of war with Imperial Germany. State Naval Militiamen, many having been trained on *Granite State (New Hampshire)* are mustered into the Navy as National Naval Volunteers.

1918
11 November
World War I ends.

1919
20 September
Independence burned on the Hunter's Point mud flats to recover her metal fittings.

1921
23 May
Granite State (New Hampshire) is severely damaged by fire, while tied to the 96th Street Pier in New York City.
19 August
The burned out hulk of *Granite State (New Hampshire)* is sold at auction for $5000 the Mulholland Machinery Corporation.

1922
July 26
Granite State (New Hampshire) catches fire while under tow, sinks off Half Way Rock in Massachusetts Bay.

1930
June
The Class of 1891 presented a bronze replica of *Delaware's* figurehead to the United States Naval Academy.

Glossary

Afore

All that part of a ship which lies forward, or near the stem. It also signified farther forward; as, the manager stands afore the foremast; that is, nearer to the stem.

Aft

Behind, or near the stern of the ship.

After

A phrase applied to any object in the hinder part of the ship, as after hatchway, the after-sails, &c.

A ground

The situation of a ship when her bottom, or any part of it, rests in the ground

All in the wind

The state of a ship's sails when they are parallel to the direction of the wind, so as to shake, or quiver.

Allowance

Stores, water, ammunition extra sails & rigging required to be carried by a ship to perform her assigned tasks.

Amidships

The middle of a ship, either with regard to her length or breadth.

Anchorage

Ground fit to hold a ship by her anchor.

At anchor

The situation of a ship riding at her anchor.

Ballast

Either is pigs of iron, stones, or gravel, which last is called single ballast; and their use is to bring the ship down to her bearings in the water which her provisions and stores will not do.

Beating to windward

The making a progress against the direction of the wind, by steering alternately close-hauled on the starboard and larboard tacks.

Between decks

The space contained between any two decks of a ship.

Bomb Ship

Also Bomb ketch, Bomb vessel, a small ketch or vessel, very strongly built, on which mortars are mounted to be used in naval shore bombardments.

Both sheets aft

The situation of a ship sailing right before the wind.

Boot-topping

Cleaning the upper part of a ship's bottom, or that part which lies immediately under the surface of the water; and paying it over with tallow, or with a mixture of tallow, sulphur, resin &c.

Boxhauling

A particular method of veering a ship, when the swell of the sea renders tacking impracticable

Bowsprit

A large piece of timber which stands out from the bows of a ship.

Breaming

Burning off the filth from a ship's bottom.

Broadside

A discharge of all the guns on one side of a ship.

Broken-backed, or hogged

The state of a ship which is so loosened in her frame as to drop at each end.

Bulwark

The sides of a ship above the decks.

By the wind

The course of a ship as nearly as possible to the direction of the wind, which is generally within six points of it.

Caliber

The diameter of a bore of a gun or cannon.

Cat-head

Large timbers projecting from the vessel's side, to which the anchor is raised and secured.

Carronade
Often referred to as a "Smasher"- A kind of short cannon, formerly in use, designed to throw a large projectile with small velocity, used for the purpose of breaking or smashing in, rather than piercing, the object aimed at, as the side of a ship. It has no trunnions, but is supported on its carriage by a bolt passing through a loop on its under side.

Carvel
In ship building, carvel is a method of constructing wooden ships by fixing planks to a frame so that the planks butt up against each other, gaining support from the frame and forming a smooth hull.

Chaser
A cannon located at the bow or stern of a vessel and used in pursuing an enemy.

Caulking
Filling the seams of a ship with oakum.

Clinker
In ship building, clinker is a method of constructing wooden ships by fixing planks to a frame so that the planks overlap each other gaining support from the frame and from adjacent planks.

Close-hauled
Trim of the ship's sails, when she endeavors to make a progress in the nearest direction possible towards that point of the compass from which the wind blows

Coppering
To cover the lower hull of a wooden ship with copper thus providing protection from aquatic wood boring worms.

Crank
A ship that demonstrates poor sailing qualities, incapable of carrying full sail without being exposed to danger.

Cruising
To sail about touching at a series of ports; sailing in search of enemy shipping.

Decommission
>To remove a ship from service

Displacement
>The weight of the water displaced by the boat

Dismasted
>The state of a sailing ship that has lost her masts.

Doubling
>The act of sailing round or passing beyond a cape or point or land.

Draft
>The depth of the boat at its lowest point, also the depth or fullness of the sail

Dry Dock
>A dock that can be kept dry for use during the construction or repairing of ships.

Driving
>The state of being carried at random, as impelled by a storm or current. It is generally expressed of a ship when accidentally broken loose from her anchors or moorings.

End-on
>When a ship advances to a shore, rock, &c. without an apparent possibility of preventing her, she is said to go END ON for the shore, &c.

Ensign
>The flag worn at the stern of a ship.

Entering-port
>A large port in the sides of three-deckers, leading into the middle deck, to save the trouble of going up the ship's side to get on board.

End-on
>When a ship advances to a shore, rock, &c. without an apparent possibility of preventing her, she is said to go END ON for the shore, &c.

Entering-port
>A large port in the sides of three-deckers, leading into the middle deck, to save the trouble of going up the ship's side to get on board.

Figurehead

Carved bust or full-length figure set at the prow of a sailing ship.

Falling off

Denotes the motion of the ship's head from the direction of the wind. It is used in opposition to Coming To.

Fall not off

The command to the steersman to keep the ship near the wind.

Fathom

A measurement relating to the depth of water, one fathom is 6 feet

Fitting Out

Readying a ship for deployment.

Flat-aft

The situation of the sails when their surfaces are pressed aft against the mast by the force of the wind.

Fleet in being

In naval warfare, a fleet in being is a naval force that extends a controlling influence without ever leaving port. Were the fleet to leave port and face the enemy, it might lose in battle and no longer influence the enemy's actions, but by simply remaining safely in port the enemy is forced to continually deploy forces to guard against it.

Flowing sheets

The position of the sheets of the principal sails when they are loosened to the wind, so as to receive it into their cavities more nearly perpendicular than when close hauled, but more obliquely than when the ship sails before the wind. A ship going two or three points large has FLOWING SHEETS.

Fore

That part of a ship's frame and machinery that lies near the stem.

Fore-and-aft

Throughout the whole ship's length. Lengthways of the ship.

Forecastle

The upper deck in the fore part of the ship.

Foremast

The mast nearest the bow of a ship

Forward

Towards the fore part of a ship.

Freeboard

The distance from the highest point of the hull to the water

Frigate

A fast square-rigged fighting ship in the 18th and early 19th centuries, next in size below a ship of the line, typically with all cannons arranged on a single covered gun deck.

Full

The situation of the sails when they are kept distended by the wind.

Full-and-by

The situation of a ship, with regard to the wind, when close-hauled; and sailing so as to steer neither too nigh the direction nor to deviate to leeward.

Grounding

The laying a ship a-shore, in order to repair her. It is also applied to running a-ground accidentally.

Gun-Deck

The deck of a sailing warship, below the main deck, where the cannons were situated

Head-sea

When the waves meet the head of a ship in her course, they are called a HEAD SEA. It is likewise applied to a large single wave coming in that direction.

Head-to-wind

The situation of a ship when her head is turned to the point from which the wind blows, as it must when tacking.

High-and-dry

The situation of a ship when so far run a-ground as to be seen dry upon the strand.

Hogging

Drooping at the ends; arching;-in distinction from sagging.

Hold

Is the space between the lower deck and the bottom of a ship and where her stores, &c. lie. To stow the hold, is to place the things in it.

Hulk

A ship without masts or rigging; also a vessel to remove masts into or out of ships by means of sheers, from whence they are called sheer hulks.

In Commission

A ship in active military service.

In Irons

Having turned onto the wind or lost the wind, stuck and unable to make headway

Jib-boom

A spar that runs out from the bowsprit.

Jurymast

Any spar that is set up, when the proper mast is carried away.

Keel

The principal piece of timber on which the vessel is built.

Knees

Are pieces of timber which confine the ends of the beams to the vessel's side.

Knot

A division of the knot-line, answering, in the calculation of the ship's velocity, to one mile.

Laid up

The situation of a ship when moored in a harbor, for want of employ.

Launch

To set a ship afloat from the building stocks.

Lazarette

Spaces below the deck that are designed for storage

Line of Battle

A formation assumed ships in preparation for combat allowing the full broadside to bear on the enemy vessels.

Log, and Log-line

By which the ship's path is measured, and her rate of going ascertained. Log-board, on which are marked the transactions of the ship, and from thence it is copied into the log-book every day.

Long-gun

In historical navy usage, a long gun was the standard type of cannon mounted by a sailing vessel, called such to distinguish it from the much shorter carronades. In informal usage, the length was combined with the weight of shot, yielding terms like "long 9s".

Mainmast

A sailing ship's principal mast usually second from the bow.

Magazine

A place where gunpowder is kept.

Manning

To supply with people (as for service) <*man* a fleet>

Masted

Having all her masts complete.

Mizzenmast

The mast aft or next aft of the mainmast in a ship

Oakum

Old rope untwisted and pulled open, used for caulking a ship.

On The Stocks

The condition of a wooden ship being constructed in the shipyard prior to launch.

Ordinary

A ship that is placed in a reduced readiness and maintenance status. "Mothballed" is the modern equivalent. Condition of long storage for possible future use.

Orlop

The lowest deck of a vessel, esp. of a ship of war, consisting of a platform laid over the beams in the hold, on which the cables are coiled.

Out-of-trim

The state of a ship when she is not properly balanced for the purposes of navigation.

Pierced

A term for gun-ports.

Poop Deck

A partial deck above a ship's main afterdeck

Port

Used for larboard, or the left side; also a harbor or haven

Quarters

The several stations of a ship's crew in time of action.

Quartering

When a ship under sail has the wind blowing on her quarter.

Quarter Gallery

A balcony on the quarter of a ship.

Rate

A ship's 'rate' was decided by the number of guns she carried, from the largest 100 or more guns first-rate, down to sixth rate 20-gun ships. The first-rate were the biggest ships of the fleet, with their gun batteries generally carried on three decks. They were generally used as flagships and fought in the center of the line-of-battle. 1st, 2nd and 3rd rated ships were deemed capable of forming the line of battle.

Razee

A razee is a sailing ship that has been cut down (razeed) to one with fewer decks. The operation was typically performed on a smaller two-deck ship of the line, resulting in a large frigate.

Receiving Ship

A receiving ship is a ship that is used in harbor to house newly recruited sailors before they are assigned to a crew.
Receiving ships were typically older vessels that could still be kept afloat, but were obsolete or no longer seaworthy. The practice was especially common in the age of wooden ships, since the old hulls would remain afloat for many years after they had become too weak to withstand the rigors of the open ocean.

Reef

Part of a sail from one row of eyelet-holes to another. It is applied likewise to a chain of rocks lying near the surface of the water.

Reefing

The operation of reducing a sail by taking in one or more of the reefs.

Reef-bands

Pieces of canvass, about six inches wide, sewed on the fore part of sails, where the points are fixed for reefing the sail.

Refit

To obtain repairs or fresh supplies or equipment.

Righting

Restoring a ship to an upright position after she has been pressed down on her side by the wind.

Road

A place near the land here ships may anchor, but which is not sheltered.

Rolling

The motion by which a ship rocks from side to side like a cradle.

Rudder

A flat piece or structure of wood or metal attached upright to the stern of a boat or ship so that it can be turned causing the vessel's head to turn in the same direction

Running Rigging

Rigging for handling sails, yards, etc. (contrasted with standing rigging). That part of a ship's rigging or ropes which passes through blocks.

Scantlings

The dimensions of the structural parts of a vessel.

Schooner

A two-masted fore-and-aft rigged vessel with a foremast and a mainmast stepped nearly amidships

Sea-boat

A vessel that bears the sea firmly, without straining her masts, &c.

Seams

The joints between the planks

Sheer

The sheer of the ship is the curve that is between the head and the stern, upon her side. The ship sheers about, that is, she goes in and out.

Shell-Gun

A cannon suitable for throwing shells. Unlike long guns, they were measured by the diameter of the shell fired, vs. the weight of the round shot.

Ship of the Line

A warship having at least two gun decks, armed powerfully enough to take a position in the line of battle. A 1st, 2nd or 3rd rate ship.

Spar Deck

The upper deck of a vessel, extending from stem to stern. Main deck.

Standing Rigging

On a sailing vessel, the standing rigging is that collection of lines which are fixed. Standing rigging includes a forestay, a backstay and the shrouds. Standing rigging is placed under tension to keep the various spars (mast, bowsprit) securely in position.

Starboard

The right-hand side of the ship, when looking forward.

Stay to

To bring the head of a ship up to the wind in order to tack.

Stem

The fore-part of the vessel.

Stern

The after-part of a vessel.

Stern Gallery

Stiff

The condition of a ship when she will carry a great quantity of sail without hazard of oversetting. It is used-in opposition to CRANK

Stores Ship

A large vessel used to transport ready to use foodstuffs and equipment, unlike a cargo ship.

Swivel Gun

A small smooth bore cannon mounted on a pedestal so that it can be turned from side to side or up and down.

Taking-in

The act of furling the sails. Used in opposition to SETTING.

Tiller

A large piece of wood, or beam, put into the head of the rudder, and by means of which the rudder is moved.

To furl

To wrap, or roll, a sail close up to the yard or stay to which it belongs, and winding a gasket round it to keep it fast.

To haul the wind

To direct the ship's course nearer to the point from which the wind blows.

To back the sails

To arrange them in a situation that will occasion the ship to move astern.

To back and fill

Is to receive the wind sometimes on the foreside of the sail, and sometimes on the other, and is used when dropping a vessel up or down a river.

To bear in with the land

Is when a ship sails towards the shore.

To bear off

To thrust or keep off the ship's side, &c. any weight when hoisting

To bear up or away

The act of changing a ship's course, to make her sail more before the wind

To becalm

To intercept the current of the wind, in its passage to a ship, by any contiguous object, as a shore above her sails, as a high sea behind, &c. and thus one sail is said to becalm another.

To brace the yards

To move the yards, by means of the braces.

To brace about

To brace the yards round for the contrary tack.

To brace sharp

To brace the yards to a position, in which they will make the smallest possible angle with the keel, for the ship to have head-way.

To brace-to

To cast off the lee braces, and round in the weather braces, to assist the motion of the ship's head in tacking.

To brail up

To haul up a sail by means of the brads.

To bring to

To check the course of a ship when she is advancing, by arranging the sails in such a manner as that they shall counteract each other, and prevent her from either retreating or advancing.

To claw off

The act of turning to windward from a lee-shore.

To club haul

A method of tacking a ship when it is expected she will miss stays on a lee-shore.

To crowd sail

To carry more sail than ordinary.

To draw

When a sail is inflated by the wind, so as to advance the vessel in her course, the sail is said TO DRAW; and SO TO KEEP ALL DRAWING is to inflate all the sails.

To fill

To brace the sails so as to receive the wind in them, and advance the ship in her course, after they had been either shivering or braced a-back.

To flat in

To draw in the aftermost lower corner or clue of a sail towards the middle of the ship, to give the sail a greater power to turn the vessel.

To flat in forward

To draw in the fore-sheet, jib-sheet, and fore-staysail-sheet, towards the middle of the ship.

To founder

To sink at sea by filling with water.

To heave to

To stop the vessel from going forward.

To labor

To roll or pitch heavily in a turbulent sea.

To lie along

To be pressed down sideways by a weight of sail in a fresh wind.

To lie to

To retard a ship in her course, by arranging the sails in such a manner as to counteract each other with nearly an equal effort, and render the ship almost immoveable, with respect to her progressive motion or headway.

To rake

To cannonade a ship at the stern or head, so that the balls scour the whole length of the decks.

To sprint a mast, yard, &c

To crack a mast, yard, &c. by means of straining in blowing weather, so that it is rendered unfit for use.

To spring a-leak

When a leak first commences, a ship is said to SPRING A-LEAK.

To stay a ship

To arrange the sails, and move the rudder so as to bring the ship's head to the direction of the wind, in order to get her on the other tack.

To strike

To lower or let down any thing. Used emphatically to denote the lowering of colors in token of surrender to a victorious enemy.

To tack

To turn a ship about from one tack to another, by bringing her head to the wind.

To tow

To draw a ship in the water by a rope fixed to a boat or other ship which is rowing or sailing on.

To veer

To change a ship's course from one tack to the other, by turning her stern to windward.

To unrig

To deprive a ship of her rigging.

To wind a ship

To change her position, bringing her head where her stern was.

To windward

Towards that part of the horizon from which the the wind blows.

To work a ship

To direct the movements of a ship, by adapting the sails, and managing the rudder, according to the course the ship lies to make.

To work to windward

To make a progress against the direction of the wind.

Trunnions of a gun

Are the arms, or pieces of iron, by which it hangs on the carriage.

Trying

The situation in which a ship, in a tempest, lies-to in the trough or hollow of the sea, particularly when the wind blows contrary to her course.

Turning to windward

That operation in sailing whereby a ship endeavors to advance against the wind.

Yawing

The motion of a ship when she deviates from to the right or left.

Water-line

The line made by the water's edge when a ship has her full proportion of stores, &c. on board.

Water-borne

The state of a ship when there is barely a sufficient depth of water to float her off from the ground.

Water-logged

The state of a ship become heavy and inactive on the sea, from the great quantity of water leaked into her.

Water-tight

The state of a ship when not leaky.

Weather

To weather any thing, is to go to windward of it.

Weather-beaten

Shattered by a storm.

Weight of Shot Thrown

The amount of round shot a ship's broadside could fire, measured in pounds. A classification of a ships offensive power.

Wind's eye

The point from which the wind blows.

Windward tide

A tide that sets to windward.

Under bare poles

When a ship has no sail set.

Bibliography

Albertson, Robert. Portsmouth Virginia. Mount Pleasant: Arcadia Publishing, 2002.

Allen, Gardner. Naval History of the American Revolution. Boston: Corner House Publications, 1970.

Besch, Michael. A Navy Second to None: The History of U.S. Naval Training in World War I (Contributions in Military Studies). Westport: Greenwood Press, 2001.

Chapelle, Howard. The History of The American Sailing Navy The Ships and their development. New York: Bonanza Books, 1988.

Chapelle, Howard. The History of American Sailing Ships. New York: Bonanza Books, 1935.

Christensen, Erwin. Early American Wood Carving. Mineola: Dover Publications, 1972.

Bonner, Kit. Warship Boneyards. Osceola: Motorbooks International, 2001.

Keatts, Henry. New England's Legacy of Shipwrecks. New York: Fathom Press, 1988.

Pictures of United States Navy ships, 1775-1941. Washington D.C.: The National Archives Trust Fund Board, 1974.

Lorenz, Lincoln. John Paul Jones: Fighter for Freedom and Glory. Annapolis: US Naval Institute, 1943.

Lyon, David. The sailing navy list: All the ships of the Royal Navy : built, purchased and captured, 1688-1860. London: Conway Maritime Press, 1993.

Morison, Samuel. John Paul Jones, A Sailor's Biography. Annapolis: Naval Institute Press September 1, 1999.

US Navy, Dictionary of American Naval Fighting Ships. Washington DC: United States Government Printing Office, 1988.

Paine, Lincoln. Ships of Discovery and Exploration. Boston: Mariner Books, 2000.

Paine, Lincoln. Warships of the World to 1900. Boston: Houghton Mifflin Company, 2000.

Roosevelt, Theodore. The Naval War of 1812. Annapolis: Naval Institute Press, 1999

Silverstone, Paul. Warships of the Civil War Navies. Annapolis: Naval Inst Press, 1989.

Vogel, Lester. To See a Promised Land: Americans and the Holy Land in the Nineteenth Century. University Park: Pennsylvania State University Press, 1993.

30th Congress, 2d Session. "House Executive Document No. 1: Message from the President of the United States." 1848: 1108-1109.

Quarterly of the National Archives and Records Administration vol. 33.no. 3 (2001).

Library of Congress, Printed Ephemera Collection; Portfolio 191, Folder 6.

Niles Weekly Register 18 March 1815.

Niles Weekly Register 25 March 1815.

"Flag lowered on oldest frigate." San Francisco Chronicle 20 November 1912.

New York Times 24 April 1921.

New York Times 27 July 1922.

Boston Globe 2 November 1965.

U.S.S. New Hampshire. Massachusetts Office of Coastal Zone Management. 24 May. 2005 <http://www.mass.gov/czm/buar/shipwrecks/ua-hampshire.htm>.

"USS Ohio Figurehead." Hercules. The Ward Melville Heritage Organization. 24 May. 2005 <http://www.wmho.org/Hercules.asp>.

About the Author

Terry Shiflett was born and raised in Stauton, the "Queen City" of Virginia's Shenandoah Valley. He has had a life long love of military history inspired by the *sea stories* told to him by his father and his father's friends. The patriotism of these World War II and Korean Conflict veterans inspired Terry to enlist in the United States Navy after completing high school. He ably served in the naval operations and intelligence fields and recently retired after twenty years of service. He now resides in Virginia Beach, Virginia with his wife, their six boys, two dogs and a cat. His "day job" is in the information technology field supporting the U.S. Navy's computer network warfare commands

www.ingramcontent.com/pod-product-compliance
Lightning Source LLC
LaVergne TN
LVHW061220060426
835508LV00014B/1378